Fade to Black

Graveside Memories of Hollywood Greats
1927 – 1950

Schiffer Publishing Ltd

4880 Lower Valley Road, Atglen, Pennsylvania 19310

Michael Thomas Barry

Author's Note

The Academy Awards for any given year are presented as follows; for example, the 1939 award ceremony was held on February 29, 1940. To avoid confusion in this book, the year cited is that of the film's release, rather than the ceremony: e.g., 1939 for *Gone with the Wind*, although it was presented its award at the 1940 event. Discussion of the actual ceremony uses the year in which the event took place. "Oscar" and "Academy Awards" are trademarks of the Academy of Motion Picture Arts and Sciences. This book is neither authorized nor endorsed by the Academy of Motion Picture Arts and Sciences.

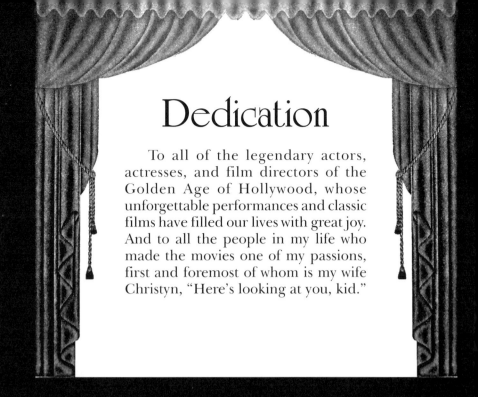

Dedication

To all of the legendary actors, actresses, and film directors of the Golden Age of Hollywood, whose unforgettable performances and classic films have filled our lives with great joy. And to all the people in my life who made the movies one of my passions, first and foremost of whom is my wife Christyn, "Here's looking at you, kid."

Back Cover Image: Celeste Holm presenting Walter Huston with his "Best Supporting Actor" Oscar at the 21st Academy Awards Ceremony, March 24, 1949. *Courtesy of the Los Angeles Public Library Collection.*

All text and photos by Michael Thomas Barry unless otherwise noted

Copyright © 2011 Michael Thomas Barry

Library of Congress Control Number: 2010941949

Designed by Mark David Bowyer
Type set in UniversityRoman Bd BT / New Baskerville BT

ISBN: 978-0-7643-3709-3

Printed in the United States of America

Schiffer Books are available at special discounts for bulk purchases for sales promotions or premiums. Special editions, including personalized covers, corporate imprints, and excerpts can be created in large quantities for special needs. For more information contact the publisher:

Published by Schiffer Publishing Ltd.
4880 Lower Valley Road
Atglen, PA 19310
Phone: (610) 593-1777; Fax: (610) 593-2002
E-mail: Info@schifferbooks.com

For the largest selection of fine reference books on this and related subjects, please visit our website at
www.schifferbooks.com
We are always looking for people to write books on new and related subjects. If you have an idea for a book please contact us at the above address.

This book may be purchased from the publisher.
Include $5.00 for shipping.
Please try your bookstore first.
You may write for a free catalog.

In Europe, Schiffer books are distributed by
Bushwood Books
6 Marksbury Ave.
Kew Gardens
Surrey TW9 4JF England
Phone: 44 (0) 20 8392-8585; Fax: 44 (0) 20 8392-9876
E-mail: info@bushwoodbooks.co.uk
Website: www.bushwoodbooks.co.uk

Contents

Acknowledgments

A project of this magnitude and scale takes many hands, eyes, and ears. To all those at Schiffer Publishing, especially Dinah Roseberry, I offer my heartfelt gratitude for giving me the opportunity to write. I also wish to express my sincere appreciation to the Academy of Motion Picture Arts and Sciences and Faye Thompson, photo archive coordinator at the AMPAS/Margaret Herrick Library. Being allowed special access to the Academy library and the opportunity to view the special collections was a priceless experience. I want to also acknowledge the Los Angeles Public Library photo archives staff and the Bruce Torrence Classic Hollywood Photo collection for their guidance and help with many of the photographs for this book. I would like to express my genuine gratitude to the Millennium Biltmore Hotel, and especially Elicia Wright at the front desk, who took the extra ordinary step of personally showing me the ballrooms where many of the actual Academy Award ceremonies took place. I express my sincere thanks to Jane Marsek at Ferncliff Cemetery, Dana Spall at Gate of Heaven Cemetery, Sleepy Hollow Cemetery, Cedar Hill Cemetery, Holy Cross and Calvary Catholic Cemeteries, who all went the extra mile in helping me to locate the famous interments at their respective properties.

Life, like the movies, is only as good as its casting. I have been fortunate to be surrounded by many supportive friends and family, but also by people who have wonderful movie memories. To Lou Carslon, thanks for planting the seed that allowed this book to grow and become reality. To Karin Billich, who helped me design my website, many thanks. To my family, wife Christyn, daughters Kate, Ashley, Allyson; my parents, Thomas (in spirit), and Dolores Barry, and my sister Laura, thanks for always being there. To the countless number of people who I have failed to acknowledge but have directly or indirectly helped make this book a reality, you have my heartfelt thankfulness. To my faithful companions, Jake and Madison, two golden retrievers, who always have a sunny attitude and have kept me companion every day while on this wondrous journey to authorship, you have helped me stay focused and grounded.

Finally, a very special acknowledgement and thank you must be extended to legendary actress, Celeste Holm. It is a tremendous honor to have an Academy Award winning actress and screen icon of her caliber review this book. Her unique perspective on the Golden Age of Hollywood is priceless and her comments will be cherished always.

Introduction

In the beginning, there was Louis B. Mayer. He looked out over his kingdom of Hollywood and its glory and said, "This is good." Then there were stirrings of unionism among the studio craftsmen and he said, "This stinks." In 1926, Hollywood was a thriving factory town and Louis B. Mayer, the head of Metro-Goldwyn-Mayer, was the big boss. The Academy of Motion Picture Arts and Sciences was born out of union turmoil. In November of 1926, all nine major Hollywood studios and five labor unions agreed on a contract. It looked as if future labor negotiations were going to be a constant headache to studio bosses, and before actors, writers, and directors got in on the action, Mayer decided to do something about it. With this union agreement only a month old, Mayer invited three of Hollywood's heavy hitters, actor Conrad Nagel, director Fred Niblo, and producer Fred Beetson to his home. These four men discussed and concocted an industry organization that would mediate labor disputes. In addition to labor disputes, the new organization would improve the industry's image by helping clean up screen content and would promote technical advances. Mayer in particular liked the idea of an elite club that would hold annual banquets. Membership would be open only to leading members of the industry's five branches: actors, directors, writers, technicians, and producers. Mayer would be in charge of picking the members. Awards were never mentioned.

On January 11, 1927, thirty-six industry leaders were invited to a formal banquet at the Ambassador Hotel in Los Angeles. Guests of this luncheon listened as Mayer extolled the virtues of the International Academy of Motion Picture Arts and Sciences. Mayer told the audience that membership in this new organization was open to those who contributed in a distinguished way to the arts and sciences of motion picture production. All thirty-six attendees signed up to be founding Academy board members. The new organization unanimously elected Louis B. Mayer, chairman of the Committee on Plan and Scope.

Mayer's lawyers immediately went to work drawing up the charter documents for the Academy. First order of business was to drop "International" from the name; it officially became the Academy of Motion Picture Arts and Sciences, and actor Douglas Fairbanks, Sr. was elected president. On May 4, 1927, the Academy became a legal corporation. On May 11, 1927, 300 invited guests attended a lavish banquet in the Crystal Ballroom at the Biltmore Hotel to celebrate; the event was paid for by Louis B. Mayer. At this affair, Academy memberships were sold for $100 apiece, and 231 guests became official members. Among the other activities at this banquet was the bestowing of "awards of merit for distinctive achievement." No one had thought beyond the concept of the award, so a Committee for the Awards of Merit was formed soon after this gathering.

A year later, in July 1928, the Awards committee finally had a voting system. Each Academy member would cast one nominating vote in his branch. Then, a Board of Judges from each branch would count the votes and determine the nominees, turning them over to a Central Board of Judges. This Central Board was comprised of one representative from each branch and these five people would pick the Academy Award winners.

Films that opened in Los Angeles between August 1, 1927 and July 31, 1928 were eligible for consideration. As the Academy members filled out their nomination ballots, the founders of the Academy deliberated over what kind of trophy, plaque, or scroll the winners would receive. Mayer left the design of the award to Cedric Gibbons (interred at Calvary Cemetery, Los Angeles, lawn H, lot 117). Gibbons came up with a design of a naked man plunging a sword into a reel of film. For production of the statuette, the Academy gave $500 to an unemployed art school graduate named George Stanley, who sculpted Gibbons' design. Alex Smith then cast the 13 ½ inch, 6 ¾ pound statuette in tin and copper and gold-plated the whole thing. The Central Board of Judges met to decide the final winners on February 15, 1929, and Louis B. Mayer was there to supervise the voting. The results of the voting were published on the back page of the Academy Bulletin on February 18, 1929. The winners were announced out right and they would receive their statuette three months later on May 16, 1929, at the Hollywood Roosevelt Hotel. The Academy Awards were born. Louis B. Mayer could not have dreamed that by concocting an organization to thwart unionism, he was creating one of Hollywood's most enduring traditions and greatest self promotional tools.

The phrase "Classical Hollywood Cinema" is universally used to represent the motion pictures from the end of the silent era until the beginning of "new" Hollywood. The actual year of which this period begins and ends is up for debate. Some film scholars place the era anywhere between 1927 and 1960. For the purpose of this book, I have chosen to use the dates of 1927 to 1950. This correlates with the establishment of the Academy Awards and finishes with the decline of the studio system in the 1950s. Film making during this period has been described as being at its most dominant, significant, and authoritative during this time. Sandwiched between the beginning of the Great Depression and the aftermath of World War II, the "golden age" arguably came at a time of great tension.

There have been countless books written about the golden age of cinema, the Academy Awards and countless biographies of major film stars of this era. My intention in writing this book is to chronicle the lives, deaths, and final resting places of the Oscar winning actors, actresses, and directors of this period. To my knowledge no other book has taken this angle in discussing this period in Hollywood history. This book is about the history of Hollywood, as reflected in the Academy Awards. Everything from the coming of sound to the rise of the various screen guilds to the impact of television to the dissolution of the studio system has had an effect on how the Oscars are distributed. History often repeats itself, and there are numerous stories about overnight successes, comebacks, pariahs and rivals in the annals of the Oscars. Many names that first appear as supporting acting candidates went on to become durable screen draws, while some top acting winners have one night of glory and are virtually never heard from again.

To some artists, the Academy Awards ritual was a silly and meaningless affair. Others have found their Oscar moment very significant and the peak professional moment of their film careers. Yet no one denies that there is an aura of fantasy about the secret envelope. As noted film director Federico Fellini remarked after winning his fourth Academy Award in 1974, "In the mythology of cinema, Oscar is the supreme prize."

I was born thirteen years after the end of the period that is covered in this book. I grew up watching movies of the late 1960s and 1970s. My early exposure to classic films was regulated to lazy Sunday afternoons or late night viewings. I liked the classic films, but an appreciation for them did not truly develop until my adult years. I have personally watched every Oscar winning movie produced during this period and after which, I truly began to understand why this era was called the "golden age" of cinema. This epoch in cinematic history was a moment in time in which sound film production rapidly developed and the art form of film making became a prominent and influential part of American culture.

This book is more than just the final resting places of the Oscar winners. The actors, actresses, and directors that I have chosen to write about all lived as we live, and their stories have needed to be told for a long time. This book is a celebration of life, not of death. Why are their lives and deaths fascinating to us? Is it that their joys, loves, triumphs, defeats, last moments, and final resting places, all encompass a life we do not have? In other words, are these people more than the granite, the marble, and the bronze markers that mark their graves? I think the answer is simply, yes. In the end, all any of us really wants is to be remembered. The cult of celebrity into which many people propel themselves today, has become a new form of religion. The searching out and visitation of the graves of famous people has become a growing past time for a large number of fans. Whatever the reason for visiting the graves of Hollywood's elite, the main enjoyment is being as close to our heroes as possible. I have personally visited most of the locations (if still standing) and final resting places discussed in this volume. They include the Roosevelt Hotel, Biltmore Hotel, Grauman's Chinese Theater, and the Pantages Theater.

It must be noted that while most cemeteries are open and welcoming to the prospect of fans visiting their favorite celebrities, a few, most notably Forest Lawn, do not allow visitors to celebrity areas, though sources note that Forest Lawn's founder, Hubert Eaton, intended a totally different experience. Eaton took control of Forest Lawn in 1917, and he coined the phrase "Memorial Park." It was Eaton's declared intention to make his cemetery a beautiful place for the "living" to visit and enjoy. He was often quoted as saying, "A cemetery should be a place of great cultural benefit for the living to sacredly enjoy." In his life time people were allowed to roam about the grounds of the memorial park unmolested. However, in the last ten years, the practice of open wandering of the grounds and mausoleums has been discontinued and the casual visitor is unfortunately no longer granted access to the "Great Mausoleum." This is a building of great beauty and is the final resting place of numerous icons of the film industry. Interred there are such legendary figures as Clark Gable, Carole Lombard, Jean Harlow, Norma Shearer, Lon Chaney, Marie Dressler, Theda Bara, David O. Selznick, Sid Grauman, and many more. Other figures such as Mary Pickford, Humphrey Bogart, Victor McLaglen, and Samuel Goldwyn are locked away in private gardens that are only accessible by key. Hubert Eaton died in 1966, and is interred within the Great Mausoleum. His crypt is among those that are no longer granted public access.

It is the hope by many that Forest Lawn will someday change policy and allow the living to once again enjoy the beauty of Forest Lawn Memorial Park, the way its founder intended.

If you do intend on visiting Forest Lawn, understand that they will not divulge any famous burial locations for you to visit. You must also remember that this is private property and as such they have the right to refuse entry and can choose to expel anyone they deem to be trespassing.

~Michael Thomas Barry
Orange, California

Chapter One
The Award Winners of the 1920s

The decade of the 1920s was a time of great contrasts. It is thought of as a hedonistic interlude book ended between the Great War and the Great Depression. It was a decade of jazz bands, raccoon coats, flappers, bootleggers, Babe Ruth, and marathon dancers. World War I had shattered American's faith in reform and morality, with this the younger generation proceeded to rebel against traditions. The "Roaring Twenties" was all this and much more, it was also the gold age of silent films; movie stars such as Mary Pickford, Douglas Fairbanks, and Charlie Chaplin ruled the box office. Looming near the end of the decade was a new technology that would transform the film business, propelling it into new direction. Talking pictures at first were a novelty and many in the business thought it was a fad. Many studio heads, and numerous actors and actresses alike never believed it could succeed. They were all wrong.

Special Note: Under the Nominees and Winners headings that follow throughout the book, the category winners are noted in bold type.

The First Academy Award Ceremony
"One Big Happy Family"

Just five short months before the Stock Market Crash of 1929 and the beginning of the Great Depression, Hollywood came together for the first time to honor its own. The first Academy Awards honoring film achievements for the years 1927 and 1928 took place on Thursday, evening May 16, 1929, at the Roosevelt Hotel in Hollywood. This ceremony was far removed from the glitzy media-heavy event that it is today and was held in the Blossom Room of the hotel. Very little attention was paid to the event by the media. This would change the following year. An Academy "member's only" event, in attendance at the banquet were 270 guests, each of whom had paid five dollars each to attend. The Blossom Room was decorated in soft light with thirty-six tables covering the entire space of the room and on each table stood a wax candy centerpiece replica of the gold award statuette.

The first organizational meeting of the Academy
of Motion Picture Arts and Sciences, Crystal
Ballroom of the Biltmore Hotel, Los Angeles,
on May 11, 1927. *Courtesy of the Herald Examiner
Collection/Los Angeles Public Library.*

There was very little suspense as to who was going to win the awards; three months earlier the winners had been announced. The master of ceremonies was the legendary screen actor and Academy President, Douglas Fairbanks. The actual presentation ceremony only lasted five minutes and as Fairbanks called out the names of the winners, each came forward and accepted their awards and then took a seat at the head table. There was only one speech that evening; it was given by Darryl F. Zanuck, who was given special recognition for producing the first talking picture, *The Jazz Singer*. The first best picture award went to *Wings*, the epic World War I spectacle. Future awards ceremonies would hold little resemblance to this first event.

The Nominees and Winners

Best Actor
Richard Barthelmess, **Emil Jannings**

Best Actress
Louise Dresser, Gloria Swanson, **Janet Gaynor**

Best Director (Drama)
King Vidor, Herbert Brenon, **Frank Borzage**

The 1st Academy Awards banquet, May 16, 1929, at the Roosevelt Hotel, Blossom Room. *Courtesy of the Bruce Torrence Hollywood photograph Collection.*

Emil Jannings

(July 23, 1884 – January 2, 1950)

Jannings was the recipient of the first Academy Award for male lead actor, and was born Theodor Friedrich Emil Janenz on July 23, 1884, in Rorschach, Switzerland. The acclaimed actor had eighty film credits between 1914 to 1945, notable motion pictures include:

- *Othello* (1922)
- *Faust* (1926)
- *Street of Sin* (1928)
- *The Patriot* (1928)
- *Betrayal* (1929)
- *The Blue Angel* (1930)

His 1929, Academy Award winning performances were for:

- *Way of the Flesh* (1927)
- *The Last Command* (1928)

Emil Jannings, 1884-1950.

Jannings did not attend the awards ceremony.

Because of his thick German accent and the advent of talking pictures, Jannings career began to wane. In the 1930s he became a supporter and activist in the Nazi party movement in Germany. He was good friends with Nazi Minister of Propaganda, Joseph Goebbels, and together made dozens of films for the Third Reich. After the end of World War II, his career never again recaptured the brilliance of his early films, and because of his pro-Nazi stance, was blacklisted from American cinema.

Emil Jannings died on January 2, 1950, at his home in Zinkenbach, Austria from liver cancer.

Emil Janning is buried at Saint Wolfgang Friedhof Cemetery, Salzburg, Austria.

Janet Gaynor

(October 6, 1906 – September 14, 1984)

Gaynor was the first winner of the Academy Award for lead actress and the youngest ever to win the award (until Marlee Matlin in 1986). She was born Laura Gainer on October 6, 1906, in Philadelphia. Gaynor had a long career in show business with over sixty film, theater, and television credits from 1924 until 1981. She was one of Hollywood's top stars from the late 1920s through the 1930s. The classic virgin-heroine type on screen, her personal life mirrored her on-screen persona. A devout Quaker, Gaynor lived at home with her mother until she got married. She was one of the few actresses to successfully move from silent pictures to talkies. Gaynor's major film credits include:

- *High Society Blues* (1930)
- *Daddy Long Legs* (1931)
- *State Fair* (1933)
- *The Farmer Takes a Wife* (1935)
- *A Star is Born* (1937)

Gaynor won the lead actress Academy award (1927-1928) for performances in three films:

- *Sunrise* (1927)
- *7th Heaven* (1927)
- *Street Angel* (1928)

During the first years of the Academy Awards, actors and actresses could win for multiple films. Gaynor's award winning performances during 1927-1928, were a real challenge to box office champ, Gloria Swanson's dominance. Gaynor was nominated for a second best actress Academy Award in 1937 in *A Star is Born*, but lost to Luise Rainer.

At the peak of her film career in 1938, Gaynor abruptly retired from films and married MGM dress designer Gilbert Adrian. Her retirement from show business lasted until 1959, when she returned to the Broadway stage in *Midnight Sun*. On September 5, 1982, Gaynor was seriously hurt in an automobile accident in San Francisco, which also injured fellow actress Mary Martin. Unfortunately, Gaynor never fully recovered from these injuries. Chronic illness followed the accident and on September 14, 1984, almost two years after the tragic car crash, Gaynor died from pneumonia at a Palm Springs, California area hospital. In accordance with her final wishes, there was no memorial or funeral service.

Janet Gaynor, 1906-1984.

Gaynor is interred at Hollywood Forever Cemetery next to her first husband, Gilbert Adrian in the Garden of Legends (formerly section 8), lot 193.

Janet Gaynor's gravesite at Hollywood Forever Cemetery.

Frank Borzage

(April 23, 1893 – June 19, 1962)

The acclaimed producer and director was born on April 23, 1893 in Salt Lake City, Utah. Borzage directed over 100 feature films from 1923 until 1961. His notable motion picture credits include:

- *Humoresque* (1920)
- *Street Angel* (1927)
- *They had to see Paris* (1929)
- *Bad Girl* (1931)
- *A Farwell to Arms* (1932)
- *Man's Castle* (1933)
- *Shipmates Forever* (1935)
- *Desire* (1936)

He won the best director Academy Award (1927-1928) for the film *7th Heaven*, starring Janet Gaynor. Borzage won a second best directing Oscar in 1931, for *Bad Girls*. He died on June 19, 1962 at his home in West Los Angeles after a long battle with cancer.

He is buried at Forest Lawn Memorial Park in Glendale, California, in the Garden of Everlasting Peace, lot 5355.

Film director, Frank Borzage's final resting place at Forest Lawn—Glendale.

The Second
Academy Awards Ceremony
"The Talkies Arrive"

The second annual Academy Awards was held on April 30, 1930, at the Ambassador Hotel, Los Angeles, in the famed Cocoanut Ballroom. The awards for film achievement covered the years 1928 and 1929. This year's event had several changes, location, more media coverage, and winners were not suppose to be revealed until the night of the awards (but this information was again, anonymously leaked out to the media prior to the ceremony). The event was broadcast for the first time over the radio. The host for the awards ceremony was the Academy of Motion Picture Arts and Sciences President, William C. DeMille. The best picture was awarded to Metro-Goldwyn-Mayer's first "talkie," *The Broadway Melody*; an extravagant song and dance film.

Did You Know?

On the evening of October 3, 1929, best actress nominee Jeanne Eagles died in New York. The actress had been suffering from the effects of alcoholism and a nervous disorder. Her death was attributed to an accidental overdose of sleep sedatives. Jeanne Eagles' final resting place is found at the East Hill Cemetery in Kansas City, Missouri.

The Nominees and Winners

Best Actor
George Bancroft, **Warner Baxter**, Chester Morris, Paul Muni, Lewis Stone

Best Actress
Ruth Chatterton, Betty Compson, Jeanne Eagles, Corrine Griffith, Bessie Love, **Mary Pickford**

Best Director
Lionel Barrymore, Harry Beaumont, Irving Cummings, **Frank Lloyd**, Ernest Lubitsch

Jeanne Eagles, 1890-1929.

Warner Baxter

(March 29, 1889 – May 7, 1951)

Warner Leroy Baxter, a handsome and dark-haired actor was one Hollywood's most successful leading men in the silent film era. He was one of only a handful of actors, who successfully transitioned from silent to talking pictures. Baxter was born March 29, 1889, in Columbus, Ohio. His film career spanned nearly four decades (1914-1950) in which he starred in over 100 motion pictures. Baxter's most famous films include:

* *The Arizona Kid* (1930)
* *Daddy Long Legs* (1931)
* *The Cisco Kid* (1931)
* *42ⁿᵈ Street* (1933)
* *Broadway Bill* (1934)
* *Under the Pampas Moon* (1935)

His 1928, Oscar winning performance was *In Old Arizona*, in which he portrayed the Cisco Kid.

In 1942, he tragically suffered a nervous breakdown. As a result, his career took a downward spiral. The studios still saw him as a viable money maker and persuaded him (after a short rest) to star in a number of "B"-level crime movie serials as "Dr. Ordway." To ease the tension on the actor, the studios imposed a maximum of two picture a year with one month film sets. This appeared to help, but by April of 1951, he had again lapsed into a painful nervous disorder. Tragically, doctors in an attempt to relieve Baxter's misery performed an ill advised lobotomy. This procedure was unsuccessful and only made his physical condition worse. Baxter was unable to eat, developed malnutrition and one month later, on May 7, 1951 at his Beverly Hills home, died from pneumonia at age fifty-eight.

On May 11, 1951, a private funeral service was held at the Christ Unity Church in Beverly Hills. In attendance were some of Hollywood's biggest film stars including; Ronald Colman, William Powell, Frank Capra, Harry Cohn, Harold Lloyd, Tyrone Power, and Darryl F. Zanuck. Following the service, Baxter's bronze casket was transported to Forest Lawn, Glendale for burial.

Warner Baxter, 1889-1951.

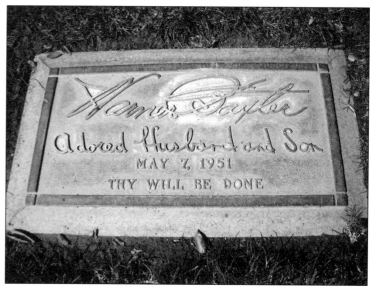

Warner Baxter's gravesite at Forest Lawn—Glendale.

Warner Baxter is buried in the Garden of Memory, crypt 579 (not far from Mary Pickford). His simple flat marker reads; "Warner Baxter (hand written style), adored husband and son, May 7, 1951, THY WILL BE DONE."

Mary Pickford

(April 8, 1892 – May 29, 1979)

"Adding sound to films would be like putting lipstick on the Venus de Milo."

~Mary Pickford

Mary Pickford was "America's Sweetheart" of the silent film era and arguably cinemas first real movie star. She was born Gladys Louise Smith on April 8, 1892, in Toronto, Canada. Her legendary career in show business began on stage at the age of five. In 1909, she appeared in her first motion picture at D.W. Griffith's film studio. Pickford's storied movie career was a relatively short twenty-four years (1909-1933). In film, she became the symbol of feminine virtue and her long curly locks were a trademark. During her prolific film career, Pickford appeared in over 240 feature films, which most notably include:

- *The Poor Little Rich Girl* (1917)
- *Rebecca of Sunnybrook Farm* (1917)
- *Daddy Long Legs* (1919)
- *Pollyanna* (1920)
- *Little Lord Fauntleroy* (1921)
- *Rosita* (1923)
- *My Best Girl* (1927)

Mary Pickford, circa 1910-1920.
Courtesy of the Library of Congress (LC-USZ62-117995)

Pickford was a bankable film star of the silent era and was also a shrewd businesswoman. In 1920, Pickford along with D.W. Griffith, Charlie Chaplin, and her future husband, Douglas Fairbanks, established the United Artists production company. She was also one of the original thirty-six founding members of the Academy of Motion Picture Arts and Sciences.

She won her first and only best actress Academy Award in 1930 for her role as Norma Besant in *Coquette* (1929). She survived damning reviews thanks to the multitudes of fans who had flocked to theaters to hear Pickford speak on film for the first time. She had appeared to have proven the critics wrong by successfully transitioning from silent films to talkies. Controversy followed the award ceremony, when it became evident that Pickford had won her award by openly campaigning for the Oscar. She had shamelessly plied voting members with lavish dinners and gifts. This prompted the academy to make changes to voting procedures, disallowing open campaigning for awards and allowing only one vote per member.

Pickford greatly underestimated the value of talking pictures, and the public failed to respond to her "talking" picture screen roles. America's love affair with Mary Pickford was at an end. She would appear in only four more films following her Oscar win in *Coquette*. In 1934, she retired from on-screen performing but continued to be a force behind the camera as a producer. In 1976, she was awarded an honorary Academy Award for lifetime achievement but was unable to attend the ceremony in person and instead sent a videotaped message of thanks.

Mary Pickford and Douglas Fairbanks at their home "Pickfair" in Beverly Hills, 1932.
Courtesy of the Herald Examiner Collection/Los Angeles Public Library

On May 25, 1979, while at her home (Pick-Fair), she became disoriented and was rushed to Santa Monica Hospital. Her condition quickly deteriorated and she slipped into a coma. Mary Pickford died on Tuesday, May 29, 1979. There was no autopsy performed but the cause of death was noted as a cerebral hemorrhage. Her simple funeral service was held at the Wee Kirk O' the Heather Chapel at Forest Lawn Glendale. In attendance were long time friend and fellow actress Lillian Gish, step son Douglas Fairbanks, Jr., and many other entertainment dignitaries but few of her contemporaries were still alive to mourn her passing. In his eulogy, film producer John Mantley (Mary's cousin) stated "I don't know what to say of a legend, it has all been said before...she was a real live vibrant human being whom the world loved...she was the essence of everything that was good and fine in the human spirit."

Pickford's cremated remains are interred in the family plot at Forest Lawn Glendale. The plot is found in the Garden of Memory, the large white marble memorial is hard to miss and is topped with ornate sculpture, her epitaph reads; "Mary Pickford Rogers, America's Sweetheart."

Mary Pickford's grave and memorial at Forest Lawn—Glendale.

Frank Lloyd

(February 2, 1888 – August 10, 1960)

Frank Lloyd was born in Glasgow, Scotland and there is much discrepancy as to exact year of his birth. Several reliable sources differ in his birth date ranging from 1886 to 1889 but his grave marker states the year as 1888. He arrived in Hollywood in 1913 and became one of the most successful directors of the silent film era.

Did You Know?
   During World War II, Lloyd was the commanding officer of the 13th Army Air Corp Combat Camera Unit and was awarded the Legion of Merit and Air Medal.

In a career that spanned forty years (1913-1955), Lloyd made over sixty feature films that included:

- *A Tale of Two Cities* (1917)
- *Les Miserables* (1917)
- *Riders of the Purple Sage* (1918)
- *The Eternal Flame* (1922)
- *Oliver Twist* (1922)
- *Within the Law* (1923)
- *Ashes of Vengeance* (1923)
- *Winds of Chance* (1925)
- *Last Command* (1955)

Lloyd was the winner of two best director Academy Awards and was nominated for a third. His first directorial Oscar was for *The Divine Lady* (1929), his second was for 1932's *Cavalcade*. In 1935, Lloyd was again nominated for an Oscar for *Mutiny on the Bounty* but lost to John Ford. Frank Lloyd died on August 10, 1960, from heart failure at St. John's Hospital in Santa Monica. His funeral service was held at the Wee Kirk O' the Heather Chapel at Forest Lawn, Glendale and in attendance were numerous Hollywood dignitaries.

Lloyd's grave is found in the Ascension lawn, lot 8438 at Forest Lawn Glendale.

Film director, Frank Lloyd's final resting place at Forest Lawn—Glendale.

The Third Academy Awards Ceremony
"Garbo Speaks"

"If only those who dream about Hollywood knew how difficult it all is."

~Greta Garbo

The third annual Academy Awards ceremony honoring film achievements (August 1, 1929 to July 31, 1930) was held on November 5, 1930, in the Fiesta Room at the Ambassador Hotel. The master of ceremonies was actor Conrad Nagel; he would host the awards ceremony three times 1930, 1932, and co-host with Bob Hope in 1953. Nagel was a prolific screen actor during the silent era, appearing in over 130 films. He was also one of the original thirty-six members of the Academy of Motion Picture Arts and Sciences.

This year's ceremony again held no suspense as to who was going to win. *Variety Magazine* was anonymously tipped off and published the winners in their morning edition. The year 1930 saw a frenzied campaign from the major studios, who shamelessly promoted their respective films and actors. MGM famously, pushed the headlines "Garbo Talks!" It was a novelty that the Academy did not fully embrace; the gravelly voiced actress Greta Garbo would finally speak in 1930's, *Anna Christie*.

This year's awards ceremony came only seven months after the previous banquet; this was due to the film industry needing to catch up after the complete transfer to talking pictures. During the ceremony, Will Hays, the former postmaster general and current industry censor, gave a one hour speech on morality and the need to cleanse the film industry. This less than enthusiastically received speech would be remembered for only one comment: Hays speaking about the state of censorship in Hollywood said "When a tree begins to collect blights, it begins to wither. So does reputation." In attendance that night was a very special honored guest, Thomas A. Edison. The best picture of the year was awarded to *All Quiet on the Western Front*. This epic film was a commentary on anti-war sentiment and portrayed the horrors of World War I.

The Nominees and Winners

Best Actor
George Arliss, Wallace Beery, Maurice Chevalier, Ronald Colman, and Lawrence Tibbett

Best Actress
Nancy Carroll, Ruth Chatterton, Greta Garbo, **Norma Shearer**, and Gloria Swanson

Best Director
Clarence Brown, Robert Leonard, Ernest Lubitsch, **Lewis Milestone**, and King Vidor

George Arliss

(April 10, 1868 – February 5, 1946)

Arliss was the best actor Academy Award winner in 1929 for *Desraeli* and *The Green Goddess*. He was the first actor to win the award for portraying the same character in film and on the stage. He was born George Augustus Andrews on April 10, 1868, in London, England. An acclaimed actor of both British and American stage and screen, he appeared in twenty-five feature films from 1921 to 1937. Arliss is best known for portraying many of the great figures in history and for his trademark monocle eye piece. Arliss' major film credits include:

- *The Millionaire* (1931)
- *Alexander Hamilton* (1931)
- *The Man Who Played God* (1932)
- *Voltaire* (1933)
- *The Iron Duke* (1934)

He died on February 5, 1946, from a bronchial ailment (presumed to be pneumonia) in London, England.

He is buried at the All Saints Churchyard Cemetery, Harrow Weald, England.

Right:
George Arliss, 1868-1946.
*Courtesy of
Library of Congress,
George G. Bain Collection
(LC-DIG-ggbain-38675)*

Norma Shearer

(August 10, 1902 – June 12, 1983)

"Never let them see you in public after you've turned thirty-five. You're finished if you do!"

~Norma Shearer

Known as the "First Lady of MGM," Norma Shearer was born Edith Norma Shearer on August 10, 1902, in Montreal, Canada. She was one of only a handful of actress to successfully transition from silent films to talkies. During a successful film career that lasted from 1919 to 1942, she appeared in sixty films. Known mainly for playing heroic and tragic roles, the versatile actress' major film credits include:

- *The Stealers* (1920)
- *The Actress* (1928)
- *The Trial of Mary Dungan* (1929)
- *Let Us Be Gay* (1930
- *A Free Soul* (1931)

- *Strange Interlude* (1932)
- *Riptide* (1934)
- *The Barrett's of Wimpole* Street (1934)
- *Romeo and* Juliet (1937)
- *Marie Antoinette* (1938)

During her long and storied film career, Shearer was nominated for six lead actress Academy Awards but won only once in 1930 for her portrayal of Jerry Martin in the *Divorcee*. That same year, she was nominated for a second lead actress award for the film, *Their Own Desire* (1929). Actress Joan Crawford's alleged reaction to Shearer's Oscar win was quite catty, "What do you expect? She sleeps with the boss!" Shearer was the wife of MGM executive Irving Thalberg.

Did You Know?

Shearer claimed to have turned down the lead role of Scarlett O'Hara in 1939's *Gone with the Wind*, but others claimed that this was not true and that David O. Selznick was forced to offer the role to Vivien Leigh after there was a public outcry against Shearer.

Norma Shearer, 1902-1983. *Courtesy of the Library of Congress, George G. Bain Collection (LC-DIG-ggbain-38806)*

From left to right, Irving G. Thalberg, Norma Shearer, and Louis B. Mayer at the premiere of *The Great Ziegfeld* on April 18, 1936. *Courtesy of the Herald Examiner Collection/ Los Angeles Public Library*

Following the death of her first husband, Irving Thalberg, in 1937, Shearer's film career began to steadily decline. She retired from film in 1942 after marrying Martin Arrouge, a young ski instructor (twenty years her junior). Shunning the limelight in her later years, she became anxious, depressed, and suicidal. The former actress spent the last years of her life locked away at the Motion Picture and Television Country Home in Woodland Hills, California. Wheel chair bound and incoherent, she died on June 12, 1983, at the country home from complications of Alzheimer's disease and pneumonia.

She is interred with her first husband, Irving Thalberg, at Forest Lawn Memorial Park, Glendale in the Great Mausoleum, Sanctuary of Benediction in the Thalberg alcove. Her crypt simply reads; Norma Arrouge.

Lewis Milestone

(September 30, 1895 – September 25, 1980)

"Everything went off fine for a couple of weeks, and suddenly we were doing a scene and Marlon spoke to the cameraman, right past me. He said: 'Look, I'll tell you, when I go like this, it means roll it, and this gesture means you stop the camera. You don't stop the camera until given the right signal.' Well, I was amazed, but didn't say anything about it."

~Lewis Milestone
on directing Marlon Brando in
Mutiny on the Bounty

The award winning film director was born Lev Milstein in Russia. Known as "Milly" to his close associates, he directed over fifty films in a career that spanned over four decades from 1918 to 1964. He was nominated for three best director Academy Awards, winning two. The first win was for *Two Arabian Knights* (1929), which was the first and only best comedy directing award ever given out. His second best directing Oscar was for 1930's, *All Quiet on the Western Front*. Other feature film credits include:

- *Front Page* 1931)
- *The General Died at Dawn* (1936)
- *Of Mice and Men* (1939)
- *A Walk in the Sun* (1945)
- *The Red Pony* (1949)
- *Les Miserables* (1952)
- *Pork Chop Hill* (1959)
- *Ocean's Eleven* (1960)
- *Mutiny on the Bounty* (1962)

Milestone died on September 25, 1980, at the UCLA Medical Center in Los Angeles from complications following an unknown surgery.

He is buried at Westwood Memorial Park in the Sanctuary of Tenderness.

Film director, Lewis Milestone's crypt at Westwood Memorial Park.

Chapter Two
The Award Winners of the 1930s

The decade of the 1920s was a time of great excess and optimism. By contrast, the 1930s were seen as a time of tremendous pain and suffering. The events of 1929 had a traumatic effect on the world and shook the foundations of American Society. The economic collapse would deepen as the decade went on and an aura of deprivation and despair would linger for almost a dozen years. In addition, conditions in Europe were worsening and this led to the rise of a group of tyrannical, authoritarian, and racist political idealists. The Nazi party in Germany, led by a fanatical leader, Adolph Hitler, would eventually ignite another world war. This was the back drop to the beginning of the Golden Age of Cinema. The down-trodden and depressed wanted relief from these troubled times and flocked to the movies. Talking pictures had finally taken over, and Hollywood would be at its pinnacle.

The Fourth Academy Awards Ceremony
"Does Size Really Matter?"

The fourth rendition of the annual awards ceremony honoring Hollywood's best films for 1930-1931 was held on November 10, 1931, at the Biltmore Hotel in Los Angeles. The evening's festivities were hosted by veteran character actor Lawrence Grant, who appeared in nearly 100 feature films from 1915 to 1945. The ceremony was filled with great confusion, the actual awards presentations did not get under way until well after midnight. *Variety Magazine* went on to call the event a "snooze and a dull evening." The guest of honor was U.S. Vice-President Charles Curtis, whose speech was long and boring and many in the audience slipped out to the lobby to partake in other frivolities. The best picture Oscar went to the epic western *Cimarron*, a tale of the famous 1889 Oklahoma land rush.

The Millennium Biltmore Hotel,
Los Angeles, present day.

The Nominee and Winners

Best Actor
Richard Dix, Jackie Cooper, **Lionel Barrymore**, Fredric March, and Adolphe Menjou

Best Actress
Marlene Dietrich, **Marie Dressler**, Irene Dunne, Ann Harding, and Norma Shearer

Best Director
Clarence Brown, Lewis Milestone, **Norman Taurog**, Wesley Ruggles, and Josef Von Sternberg

Lionel Barrymore

(April 12, 1878 – November 15, 1954)

"Half the people in Hollywood are dying to be discovered and the other half are afraid they will be."

~Lionel Barrymore

Lionel Barrymore was born on April 12, 1878 in Philadelphia. The celebrated actor was the patriarch of the fabled Barrymore acting family, which included his siblings John and Ethel. Lionel's storied film career included over 200 films that spanned four decades (1911 to 1954). The versatile actor was best known for playing grouchy, lovable, elderly man. His major film credits include:

- *Mata Hari* (1931)
- *Grand Hotel* (1932)
- *Treasure Island* (1934)
- *Captains Courageous* (1937)

He starred only once with his three famous siblings in 1932's *Rasputin and the Empress*. He is best known for his role as Mr. Potter in Frank Capra's, *It's a Wonderful Life* (1946) and as Dr. Leonard Gillespie in the *Doctor Kildare* serials. His Oscar award-winning performance as the booze guzzling lawyer who saves Clark Gable's neck and then has to defend his son-in-law for killing Gable in *A Free Soul* is arguably not his best performance. Crippled by arthritis and a hip injury from 1938 until his death in 1954, his screen roles were written to accommodate his wheelchair disability. Despite this handicap, he still became one the most successful actors of the 1940s and early 1950s.

Right:
Lionel Barrymore, 1878-1954.

Lionel Herbert Barrymore died on November 15, 1954, at the Valley Hospital in Van Nuys, California. He was stricken with a heart attack the night before at the home he shared with a friend in Chatsworth. Barrymore had suffered from a congestive heart condition for many years prior to his death. The patriarch of the royal family of the American theater's funeral mass was held in the chapel at the Calvary Cemetery on November 18, 1954. Many of Hollywood's elite were in attendance, including Frank Capra, Bing Crosby, Spencer Tracy, and Mickey Rooney. There were forty-eight honorary pall bearers that included Clark Gable, Bob Hope, and Louis B. Mayer.

Barrymore is interred in the "royal family" crypt which is located in the main mausoleum, block 352 of Calvary Catholic Cemetery in East Los Angeles.

Just beneath Lionel's crypt is the former final resting place of his brother, John Barrymore. In the early 1980s, John's family had his remains removed, cremated, and reburied with his parents at Mount Vernon Cemetery in Philadelphia. The crypt remains empty today but still bears the legendary actor's name and epitaph "good night sweet prince." Their sister Ethel Barrymore is also interred at Calvary Cemetery.

Lionel Barrymore's crypt at Holy Cross Catholic Cemetery, Los Angeles.

Marie Dressler

(November 9, 1868 – July 28, 1934)

"I contend that every woman has the right to feel beautiful, no matter how scrambled her features, or how indifferent her features."

~Marie Dressler

Marie Dressler was born Leila Marie Koerber in Canada and she was one of the top box office draws of the early 1930s. Her self-styled image as the frumpy, matronly, ugly duckling in many of her films allowed her to soar to the heights of stardom that would culminate with an Academy Award for best actress in 1931. Dressler began her career in film in 1914 in a Mack Sennett comedy entitled, *Tillie's Punctured Romance*. Appearing with her in this film were two yet unknown actors, Charlie Chaplin and Mabel Normand, who would go on to fame of their own.

By 1918, Dressler's career in film was drastically in decline. Hollywood has few roles for an aging actress and by the end of the 1920s, she was near poverty and practically homeless. Miraculously, an angel appeared to rescue her career; Irving Thalberg at MGM saw potential and set out to make her a star. She appeared in twenty-nine films from 1914 to 1933; major film credits include:

- *Anna Christie* (1930)
- *Emma* (1932)
- *Dinner at Eight* (1933)
- *Tugboat Annie* (1933)

Dressler won the 1931 Academy Award for the her portrayal of Min Divot in *Min and Bill*. She was nominated the following year for a second best acting award for *Emma* (1932) but lost to Helen Hayes. It was the homely Marie Dressler, who won the coveted exhibitor's poll as the most popular actress three years in a row (1931-1933), beating out beauties such as Greta Garbo, Jean Harlow, and Joan Crawford.

In the midst of her fame, Dressler was quoted as saying, "Middle age is the best part of life, you don't really begin to live or to appreciate life until after you're 50." As she was just reaching the zenith of her success in film and after signing a long term contract with MGM, doctors informed her that she had an advanced case of stomach cancer. The prognosis was not good and she quickly faded away. After slipping into a coma, the actress died on July 28, 1934 at her Montecito, California, estate, surrounded by family and friends. The immediate cause of death was uremia (failure of the kidneys), complicated by congestive heart failure and cancer. Dressler's funeral was held on July 31, 1934 in the Wee Kirk O' the Heather Chapel at Forest Lawn Memorial Park, Glendale. In attendance were 150 family, friends, and Hollywood notables that included Lionel Barrymore. Close friend and fellow actress Jeanette MacDonald sang during the service.

Dressler is interred within the Great Mausoleum at Forest Lawn Glendale in the Sanctuary of Benediction.

Interior view of the Sanctuary of Benediction at Forest Lawn – Glendale, circa mid-1950s. The iron doors directly at the end of the sanctuary marks the entrance to the Thalberg alcove where the remains of Irving Thalberg and Norma Shearer are interred. To the left of the iron doors, may be seen the "Statue of Curiosity," which enshrouds the private room where Jean Harlow is entombed. The third crypt from the bottom in the first tier of the third section from the entrance of the sanctuary is the final resting place of Marie Dressler. *Courtesy of the Los Angeles Public Library*

Norman Taurog

(February 23, 1899 – April 7, 1981)

Norman Taurog, an award-winning film director, who built a reputation in Hollywood for his affinity for animals and children was born on February 23, 1899, in Chicago, Illinois. His film career spanned four decades from 1920-1964 and included over 170 motion pictures. Known affectionately as "Uncle Norman" to child stars such as Judy Garland and Mickey Rooney, he attributed his success to "never asking a child actor to do anything I wouldn't ask a child of my own to do." His famous five rules for guiding child actors were: Never lose your patience. Never raise your voice. The director is responsible for the picture, not the parents. Never show the actor how to enact a scene, and win their confidence by treating them as you would treat grown-ups. These rules led to his great success in the industry.

Taurog's major film credits include:

- *Trooper's Three* (1930)
- *The Adventures of Tom Sawyer* (1938)
- *Broadway Melody of 1940* (1940)
- *Room for One More* (1952)

He also directed nine movies (most of any other director) starring Elvis Presley that included:

- *G.I. Blues* (1960)
- *Blue Hawaii* (1961)
- *Spin Out* (1966)
- *Live a Little, Love a Little* (1968)

Taurog won the best directing Oscar in 1931 for the film *Skippy*, starring his nephew and best actor nominee Jackie Cooper. He was again nominated for a best directing award in 1938 for the film *Boy's Town* but lost to Frank Capra. On April 7, 1981, at the Eisenhower Medical Center, Rancho Mirage, California, the beloved director died after battling a lengthy and undisclosed illness.

Norman Taurog's remains were cremated and his ashes were scattered at sea by family members.

The Fifth Academy Awards Ceremony
"It's a Tie"

Covering films of 1931 and 1932, the awards show was held on November 18, 1932, at the Ambassador Hotel. Conrad Nagel again reprised his post as master of ceremonies. The evening was filled with many surprises and a few unforgettable quotes. During the presentations Lionel Barrymore, the best actor winner from the previous year gave an impassioned speech on the integrity of the Academy voting process. The irony of his remarks were realized a short time later when for the first time in the awards short history, there was a tie (actually a one vote separation) in voting for best actor. The best picture award went to *Grand Hotel* starring Greta Garbo, in which she said the immortal line, "I vant to be alone."

The Nominees and Winners

Best Actor
Wallace Beery, **Fredric March**, and Alfred Lunt

Best Actress
Marie Dressler, Lynn Fontanne, and **Helen Hayes**

Best Director
Frank Borzage, King Vidor, and Josef Von Sternberg

Wallace Beery

(April 1, 1885 - April 15, 1949)

Wallace Beery, the lovable old rascal and veteran actor of 230 motion pictures was born on April 1, 1885 (the actual year varies with different sources), in Kansas City, Missouri. A man's man, he stood 6'1", with a bulky frame and husky, booming voice. His big break in show business came in 1915, that same year he met and married his first wife, a very young Gloria Swanson. The marriage only lasted three years; Swanson tired of Beery's abusive behavior and heavy drinking and the couple divorced in 1919.

On film, he was known as the actor with the rough hewn exterior with a sentimental streak. In real life he was nothing like the lovable slobs he played on screen. Beery's film career spanned nearly thirty years from 1915 to 1949; major film credits include:

- *The Sea Hawk* (1924)
- *The Pony Express* (1925)
- *Behind the Front* (1926)
- *The Big House* (1930)
- *Min and Bill* (1930)
- *Dinner at Eight* (1933)
- *Treasure Island* (1934)
- *Wyoming* (1940)

Publicity still for The Bowery, left to right: George Raft, Jackie Cooper, and Wallace Beery. (20th Century Fox, 1933).

The gravesite of actor Wallace Beery at Forest Lawn—Glendale.

Did You Know?
At the age of sixteen, Beery was employed by Ringling Brothers Circus as an elephant trainer. He also turned down the role of the wizard/professor in MGM's *The Wizard of Oz* (1939) due to other contractual obligations.

He was nominated for a best actor Oscar in 1930 for *The Big House* losing to George Arliss, but won the award in 1932 for *The Champ*. Beery had actually lost to Fredric March by one vote but a loophole in Academy rules stated that if in the event of a vote of three or less, a tie could be declared. At the ceremony, host Conrad Nagel took it upon himself (with much controversy and no authority) to declare the tie and handed two awards out for best actor. Prior to the awards ceremony, it is alleged that Beery, upon hearing the advance news that he had lost to Fredric March, stormed into the office of MGM boss Louis B. Mayer and demanded that the award be given to him. Mayer apparently relented and forced a tie in the voting to satisfy his box office star. This controversy caused the Academy to change the rules yet again, the following year and thereafter, no ties would be declared unless it was an actual situation where the votes were equal. The accounting firm of Price-Waterhouse would tabulate and collect the secret ballots to prevent fraud from here on out.

Beery died on April 15, 1949, at his home in Beverly Hills, California, of a heart attack. He had suffered from heart troubles for some time and had been confined to his home when he was stricken. A private funeral service was held at the Church of the Recessional at Forest Lawn Memorial Park, Glendale; in attendance were many Hollywood notables, including Louis B. Mayer, Clark Gable, Mack Sennett, and Darryl F. Zanuck.

Wallace Beery is buried at Forest Lawn, Glendale in the Vale of Memory lawn, lot 2086. His epitaph reads; "No man is indispensable but some are irreplaceable."

Fredric March

(August 31, 1897 – April 14, 1975)

The two-time Academy Award winning actor was born Fredrick McIntyre Bickel on August 31, 1897, in Racine, Wisconsin. His film career began inauspiciously in 1920 as a film extra, but by 1926, he had become a full-fledged star of the Broadway stage. He was a well-respected actor who appeared in eighty-four films and television programs in a film career that spanned five decades (1920 to 1973). March was known primarily as the suave, romantic leading man in many of his films; he broke tradition for his first Academy Award winning role, (he shared the award with fellow actor Wallace Beery) playing the diabolical Mr.Hyde in 1932's *Dr. Jekyll and Mr. Hyde*. He would go on to win another best acting Oscar in 1947 for the film, *The Best Years of Our Lives*. He was nominated for three additional best acting Oscar's in 1930, 1938, and 1952 but lost each time. March's other notable film credits include:

- *The Royal Family of Broadway* (1930)
- *All of Me* (1934)
- *Death Takes a Holiday* (1934)
- *Anna Karenina* (1935)
- *A Star is Born* (1937)
- *The Buccaneer* (1938)
- *Death of a Salesman* (1951)
- *The Bridges of Toko-Ri* (1954)
- *Inherit the Wind* (1960)

He was also the recipient of two Tony Awards for best acting in 1947 and 1957. Fredric March died on April 14, 1975, at Mount Sinai Hospital in Los Angeles from prostate cancer.

Fredric March is buried at his family estate in New Milford, Connecticut.

Fredric March as Mr. Hyde in *Dr. Jekyll & Mr. Hyde*
(Paramount Pictures publicity still, 1932.)

Fredric March, circa 1939. *Courtesy of the Library of Congress,*
Carl Van Vechten Collection (LC-USZ62-103668)

Helen Hayes

(October 10, 1900 – March 17, 1993)

"Age is not important unless you're a cheese."
~Helen Hayes

Helen Hayes known as "the First Lady of the American theater" was born Helen Hayes Brown on October 10, 1900, in Washington, District of Columbia. The diminutive star was an award winning actress of stage, film, and television. Her show business career spanned seven decades from 1931 to 1985. Hayes had a very disciplined stage technique but was never totally at ease in Hollywood or with the star system. As a result she never fully embraced the screen but she adored the theater. Although her film appearances were few in quantity they were almost always high in quality. Her major film credits include:

- *Arrowsmith* (1931)
- *A Farewell to Arms* (1932)
- *Another Language* (1933)
- *Night Flight* (1933)
- *Crime Without Passion* (1934)
- *Vanessa: Her Love Story* (1935)
- *Airport* (1970)

She won two Academy Awards, first in 1932 for best actress, playing the role of a prostitute in *The Sin of Madelon Claudet* (1931), which was her debut on the big screen. A second Oscar win was for best supporting actress and it came forty years later, in 1970's *Airport*. She was nominated for numerous other awards including nine Emmy awards (winning one), two Golden Globes, and three Tony Award wins.

Helen Hayes died on March 17, 1993, at the Nyack Hospital in Nyack, New York, from heart failure at age ninety-two. Her funeral was held at St. Ann's Catholic Church in Nyack. The funeral mass was attended by nearly 500 mourners and was officiated by Cardinal John J. O'Connor.

Helen Hayes is buried in a simple grave at the Oak Hill Cemetery in Nyack, New York.

The 1932 award-winning director **Frank Borzage's** life, film career, and final resting place are discussed in "The First Oscar Ceremony" in chapter one.

Right:
Helen Hayes, 1900-1993, circa 1920s.

The Sixth Academy Awards Ceremony
"A Tale of Two Franks"

The sixth installment of Hollywood's grand evening of self congratulation was held on March 16, 1934, and for a second consecutive year at the Ambassador Hotel. The awards ceremony honoring the films of 1932 and 1933 came a short seventeen months after the last gathering (a result of the Academy needing to catch up). The host for the evening was humorist and political activist, Will Rogers. All night the satirist poked fun at politicians, the Hollywood elite, and even the past controversies of the Oscars themselves. Roger's wry sense of humor caused one the more embarrassing moments in Oscar history. While presenting the best director award, Rogers preplanned a prank, in which he would only announce the first name of the winner, that being "Frank." Rogers after opening the envelope said, "It couldn't have happened to a nicer guy. Come up and get it Frank!" There was one problem; there were two Franks nominated, Frank Capra and Frank Lloyd. Upon hearing the name, assuming it was he, who had won; Frank Capra leaped to his feet in joyous celebration and strode triumphantly toward the podium to accept his award. Unfortunately, and most embarrassingly for Capra, Frank Lloyd was the actual winner, the spot light turned toward Lloyd and Capra half way down the aisle, sheepishly slinked back to his table. An anonymous person in the crowd sarcastically yelled, "down in front." The year's best picture category was filled with some of Hollywood's most memorable classics and *Cavalcade* came out on top as the year's best film, taking home three awards for best picture, best director, and best art design.

The Nominees and Winners

Best Actor
Leslie Hunt, Paul Muni, and **Charles Laughton**

Best Actress
May Robson, **Katharine Hepburn**, and Diana Wynyard

Best Director
Frank Lloyd, George Cukor, and Frank Capra

Charles Laughton

(July 1, 1888 – December 15, 1962)

"Method actors give you a photograph. Real actors give you an oil painting."

~Charles Laughton

Charles Laughton, a star of both stage and screen, was born on July 1, 1899, at the Victoria Hotel in Scarborough, England. This small establishment was owned by his parents. In 1924, at the age of twenty-five, Laughton entered the acclaimed acting school at the Royal Academy of the Dramatic Arts in London, studying under the famed, Alice Gachet; she told him, "I will make you an actor," and she did.

Both hated and loved during his acting career, Laughton's dual personalities allowed him to play a wide variety of versatile roles. He could play the majestic, angry, sinister, lovable, sarcastic, and comedic very well. Laughton was well aware of his less than dashing looks, he often sarcastically said, "I have a face that would stop a sun dial and frighten small children."

Right:
Charles Laughton, 1888-1962.

Yet screen beauty Marlene Dietrich once said, "I would rather play a love scene with Charles Laughton than any other man in the world."

His film career spanned thirty-plus years (1928 to 1962) and included sixty-five major motion pictures. Some of his most famous film credits include:

- *Les Miserables* (1935)
- *Mutiny on the Bounty* (1935)
- *Rembrandt* (1936
- *The Hunchback of Notre Dame* (1939)
- *The Canterville Ghost* (1944)
- *Captain Kidd* (1945)
- *The Girl from Manhattan* (1946)
- *Witness for the Prosecution* (1957)
- *Spartacus* (1960)

Laughton was nominated for three best acting awards, 1934, 1936, and 1958, winning in 1934 for his portrayal of the gluttonous monarch, Henry VII in *The Private Lives of Henry VIII* (1933).

Laughton died on December 15, 1962, at his Hollywood Hills home of spinal cancer. He had suffered for nearly a year with the disease, undergoing several surgeries that left him basically bedridden. His funeral was held on December 19, 1962, at the Church of the Hills at Forest Lawn Memorial Park, Hollywood Hills. In attendance were numerous Hollywood notables that included Oscar winning actress Norma Shearer. The eulogy was given by author Christopher Isherwood; in his speech he praised Laughton for his great acting genius and for his inspiration to young actors. Isherwood read from Shakespeare, "our revels are now ended. These our actors, as I foretold you were all spirits, and are melted into air thin air…" a fitting farewell to an accomplished actor.

Laughton's final resting place at Forest Lawn, Hollywood Hills is located in the Court of Remembrance, crypt C-310.

Right:
Charles Laughton's crypt at Forest Lawn—Hollywood Hills.

Katharine Hepburn

(May 12, 1907 – June 29, 2003)

"The average Hollywood film star's ambition is to be admired by an American, courted by an Italian, married to an Englishman, and have a French boyfriend."

~Katharine Hepburn

The first lady of American cinema, Hepburn was born on May 12, 1907 in Hartford, Connecticut. Her father, Thomas Houghton Hepburn, was a prominent surgeon and her mother, Katharine Martha Houghton, was a renowned suffragette. The actress had strong family ties and spoke highly of her parents; she is quoted as saying "the single most important thing anyone needs to know about me is that I am totally, completely the product of two damn fascinating individuals who happen to be my parents." Her upper-class upbringing helped with her on-screen character development; she often played the femme fatale or the slightly pretentious woman on a mission. She was a very unique person, head strong with plenty of arrogance that went against the traditional Hollywood starlet mold.

Her legendary film career spanned six decades (1932-1994), with over fifty feature motion picture credits. Hepburn was the winner of four best actress Academy Awards:

- *Morning Glory* (1932)
- *Guess Who's Coming to Dinner* (1967)
- *The Lion in Winter* (1968)
- *On Golden Pond* (1981)

Hepburn was also nominated for eight additional best actress awards:

- *Alice Adams* (1935)
- *The Philadelphia Story* (1940)
- *Woman of the Year* (1942)
- *The African Queen* (1951)
- *Summer Time* (1955)
- *The Rainmaker* (1956)
- *Suddenly, Last Summer* (1959)
- *Long Day's Journey into Night* (1962)

Did You Know?

Hepburn was a graduate of Bryn Mawr College (1928) with degrees in history and philosophy. She is quoted as saying that she never watched *Guess Who's Coming to Dinner*, because it was Spencer Tracy's last film and it would have been too emotional.

Right:
Katharine Hepburn, 1907-2003.

Romantically, Hepburn was linked to many of the leading men of the era, they included; Howard Hughes, Leland Howard, and the self-professed love of her life Spencer Tracy. The on and off screen chemistry between Tracy and Hepburn was very apparent in the nine films in which they both starred. Tracy was a married man who never divorced his wife because of his devout Catholicism. Hepburn and Tracy's unconventional twenty-seven year romance ended with his death in 1967. In her 1991 memoir, Hepburn wrote about the romance, "I have no idea how Spence felt about me. I can only say, I think that if he hadn't liked me, he wouldn't have hung around. As simple as that. He wouldn't talk about it, and I didn't talk about it. We just passed twenty-seven years together in what was to be absolute bliss. It is called LOVE."

One of the last true, iconic legends of the golden age of cinema, Hepburn died on June 29, 2003, at her home in Sunnybrook, Connecticut, from complications of Parkinson's disease and old age. A notoriously private person in life, her funeral was a private affair.

Katharine Hepburn is buried in the family plot with her parents and other siblings at Cedar Hill Cemetery in Hartford, Connecticut, section 10.

Frank Lloyd

The life, career and final resting place of the 1933 best director award winner, Frank Lloyd is discussed in chapter one.

The Hepburn family burial plot at Cedar Hill Cemetery with actress Katharine Hepburn's grave marker in the foreground center.

Actress Katharine Hepburn's grave marker at Cedar Hill Cemetery.

The Seventh Academy Awards Ceremony
"It's a Sweep"

The seventh rendition of Academy Awards honoring films from 1934 were held on February 27, 1935 at the Biltmore Hotel in Los Angeles, California. In attendance were a record 1,000 attendees and the master of ceremonies for the evening's event was author and humorist Irvin S. Cobb. The best picture of the year, *It Happened One Night* won all five major categories including Best picture, actor, actress, director, and screen play. This was the first time a film had garnered all the top honors. Also, popular child star, Shirley Temple received an honorary miniature Oscar for her contributions to film.

The Nominees and Winners

Best Actor
Frank Morgan, **Clark Gable**, and William Powell

Best Actress
Norma Shearer, **Claudette Colbert**, and Grace Moore

Best Director
W.S. Van Dyke, **Frank Capra**, and Victor Schertzinger

Clark Gable
(February 1, 1901 – November 16, 1960)

"Hell, if I jumped all the dames I'm supposed to have jumped on, I'd have had no time to go fishing."
~Clark Gable

The "King of Hollywood," William Clark Gable, was born on February 1, 1901, in Cadiz, Ohio. His mother, Adeline, died when Clark was only seven months old. The acting bug struck Gable when he was fifteen and working as an errand boy at the Akron Theater, but this foray into the entertainment industry was short lived, after the death of his step mother; his father moved the family to Oklahoma, where the young Gable worked as a roustabout in the oil fields. Determined to be a star, and against his father's wishes, Clark left Oklahoma for a job as a stage hand at a small theater in Portland, Oregon. It was there that he met his future wife, Josephine Dillon, a well known Broadway actress. She tutored Clark and brought him to Los Angeles, where they were married on December 13, 1924; the pair would divorce six years later.

Right:
Clarke Gable with his Oscar at the 7th Academy Awards banquet, February 27, 1935.
Courtesy of the Los Angeles Public Library

Gable had arrived in the city where he would become a legend. His big break came when veteran actor Lionel Barrymore spotted the young actor in a play and got him several bit parts in movies. Director, Darryl F. Zanuck's first impression of the young star was brutally honest but very wrong. Speaking to Gable he said, "Buddy, your ears are too big. You'll never make it." The famed director was being candid but wrong. In the 1931 film, *The Free Soul*, Gable played a gangster, who roughs up actress Norma Shearer's character. The studio heads, including Louis B. Mayer, thought this would repulse female film goers but it did not, the film made Clark Gable a star. During his time in Hollywood, Gable was the undisputed "king of the movies," a box office leader, forty-one of his film's would gross over sixty-three million dollars and he was reportedly paid more than $48,000 a week on a film set.

Gable's film career spanned nearly four decades from 1923 to 1961, he appeared in eighty-one films some of which included:

- *Hell Divers* (1931)
- *Strange Interlude* (1932)
- *Manhattan Melodrama* (1934)
- *Wife vs. Secretary* (1936)
- *San Francisco* (1936)
- *They Met in Bombay* (1941)
- *Across the Wide Missouri* (1951)
- *Band of Angels* (1957)

He was nominated for three best acting Oscars, his first and only win was in 1934's, *It Happened One Night;* he was nominated but lost in 1936 for *Mutiny on the Bounty,* and 1940 playing the legendary role of Rhett Butler in *Gone with the Wind.*

In 1932 on the set of the film, *No Man of Her Own,* Clark Gable met the love of his life, Carole Lombard. Their first meeting was uneventful, and did not leave a lasting impression. Years later, in 1936 at a Hollywood party, the pair were again united and hit it off. There was one hitch, the two movie stars were still married, Lombard to Robert Powell and Gable to Maria Langham. This minor detail did not stop the pair from seeing one another and a scandalous affair ensued. The two eventually got divorces from their respective spouses and married on March 29, 1939, during a break in the filming of *Gone with the Wind.* During his marriage to Lombard, Gable has been characterized as being at his happiest. Carole Lombard's youthful, yet blunt personality was a good match for Gable. Tragedy struck on January 16, 1942, when Lombard was killed in plane crash, while on a war bond publicity drive. This devastated Gable, and although he would go on

to make an additional twenty-seven films, he was never emotionally the same person.

On the late evening of November 16, 1960, at Hollywood Presbyterian Hospital in Los Angeles, the legendary actor died of a heart attack. He had just wrapped up filming *The Misfits,* co-starring Marilyn Monroe, when he was stricken by a minor heart condition. He returned home immediately and appeared to be recovering when the fatality occurred. His death is alleged to have been caused by extreme physical exertion and tension on the set of the film. At the time of his death, his fifth wife Kay was five months pregnant. On March 20, 1961, she gave birth to a boy, John Clark Gable.

Gable's private funeral was held at the Church of the Recessional at Forest Lawn Memorial Park in Glendale, where numerous Hollywood notables were present; pallbearers were Jimmy Stewart, Spencer Tracy, and Robert Taylor. Gable was accorded full military honors for his military service during World War II.

Gable's widow, Kay, consented to his burial beside his third wife, actress Carole Lombard, and the two are forever interred beside one another in the Great Mausoleum at Forest Lawn in the Sanctuary of Trust.

Claudette Colbert

(September 13, 1903 – July 30, 1996)

"The casting couch? There's only one of us who ever made it to stardom without it, and that was Bette Davis."
~Claudette Colbert

The versatile and award-winning actress was born Lily Claudette Chauchoin on September 13, 1903, in Saint-Mande, France. At an early age the actress and her family immigrated to the United States, settling in New York City. Her career in show business began on the stage, where her big break on Broadway came in 1927, playing the role of the snake charmer in *The Barker.* This success led directly to film contracts and a role in the 1927 silent film, *For the Love of Mike.* With the advent of talking pictures, there was a need for classically trained stage actresses and Colbert abandoned the stage for the big screen. She appeared in seventy-nine films and television programs from 1927 to 1987; film highlights include:

- *The Smiling Lieutenant* (1931)
- *The Wiser Sex* (1932)

- *The Sign of the Cross* (1932)
- *Cleopatra* (1934)
- *Imitation of Life* (1934)
- *The Gilded Lily* (1935)
- *Arise My Love* (1940)
- *No Time for Love* (1943)
- *Three Came Home* (1950)

In the early years of her career, Colbert was type cast as the sweet and virtuous woman. This image changed in 1932, and in one memorable scene from the film, *The Sign of the Cross*, Colbert playing the role of the seductress takes a scandalous dip in a bath tub filled with milk. This role helped propel her into a new category of super stardom, that of sex symbol. She was nominated for three best actress awards, *Private World's* (1935), and *Since You Went Away* (1945), but her only Academy Award win was in 1934's *It Happened One Night*, co-starring Clark Gable. Ironically, the night of her biggest success might never have been; Colbert had not planned on attending the ceremony. She believed that actress Bette Davis (due to a ground swell of last minute write-in votes) would win the award, and not wanting to be humiliated, had planned a trip to New York instead of attending the ceremony. While awaiting her train at Union Station in Los Angeles, friends of Colbert's arrived at the train station just in time to whisk the actress back to the Biltmore Hotel (under police escort) to receive the best actress Oscar. She made it just in time to accept the award and then quietly slipped out of the ballroom and resumed her planned trip to New York. As her film career began to wane in the early 1950s, Colbert made the successful switch to television and theater. She appeared on numerous television programs until 1987, and also made several successful Broadway stage appearances in the 1960s and again in the early 1980s.

The legendary actress suffered a series of strokes in March of 1993, which left her partially paralyzed and confined to a wheelchair. Despite these disabilities, Colbert continued to have a zest for life, visiting often with family and friends. On July 30, 1996, three years after her first stroke, she tragically suffered another massive stroke and died at her vacation home in Bridgetown, Barbados, at age ninety.

Claudette Colbert is buried at the Parish of Saint Peter's Cemetery in Barbados.

Claudette Colbert,
1903-1996.

Frank Capra

(May 18, 1897 – September 3, 1991)

"Script writing is the toughest part of the whole racket, the least understood and the least noticed."

~Frank Capra

The multi-talented award-winning film director, producer and writer, Frank Rosario Capra was born on May 18, 1897, in Bisacquino, Sicily, Italy. He immigrated to the United States in 1903 at the age of five with his family. Capra is best known for directing the classic holiday film, *It's a Wonderful Life* (1946), starring Jimmy Stewart.

Did You Know?
Capra was the host of the 1936 and 1939 Academy Awards ceremony, was president of the Directors Guild of America from 1939 to 1941, and was President of the Motion Pictures Arts and Sciences from 1935 to 1939.

The award-winning director's career in show business spanned nearly four decades from 1922 to 1977, in which he directed fifty-three films. In the mid-1920s, he worked for Hal Roach as a writer on numerous *Our Gang* serials, and was also employed by Mack Sennett's studio. Harry Cohn the head of Columbia Studios saw that Capra had what it took to be a star director in Hollywood and gave him support in his early films. Capra was nominated for six best director Oscars, first in 1934 for:

- *Lady for a Day, Mr. Smith Goes to Washington* (1940)
- *It's a Wonderful Life* (1947)

...and won three times:

- *It Happened One Night* (1934)
- *Mr. Deeds Goes to Town* (1935)
- *You Can't Take It with You* (1939)

Other notable film credits include:

- *Broadway Bill* (1934)
- *Lost Horizon* (1937)
- *Meet John Doe* (1941)
- *Arsenic and Old Lace* (1944)
- *Pocket Full of Miracles* (1961)

He was a master at capturing on film the social ills of the era, and with humor was able to create powerful characters who came from humble surroundings who took on society's wrongs. His films appealed to the masses of the day and also stand the test of time today as beloved classics. Frank Capra died on September 3, 1991 from a heart attack at his home in La Quinta, California.

Capra is buried in a non-descript grave at the Coachella Valley Public Cemetery in Coachella, California, block 77, lot 289, space 8.

Right:
Frank Capra's gravesite at the Coachella Valley Public Cemetery.

FRANK CAPRA
1897 — 1991

The Eighth Academy Awards Ceremony
"The Academy Throws a Party and No One Shows Up"

This year's awards show honoring film achievement for the year 1935 was held on March 5, 1936, at the Biltmore Hotel and hosted by Frank Capra. Due to a boycott of the event by the directors, actors and Writers' Guilds, few stars showed up for the gala event. This happened because of the Academy's unwillingness to intervene on behalf of the unions with regard to employment terms with the studios; the unions no longer trusted the Academy, and members were encouraged to boycott the Oscars. The best picture of the year was *Mutiny on the Bounty*, starring Clark Gable and Charles Laughton; this film had beaten the odds on favorite, *The Informer*.

The Nominees and Winners

Best Actor
Clark Gable, Charles Laughton, **Victor McLaglen**, and Franchot Tone

Best Actress
Elizabeth Bergner, Claudette Colbert, **Bette Davis**, Katharine Hepburn, Miriam Hopkins, and Merle Oberon

Best Director
John Ford, Henry Hathaway, and Frank Lloyd

Victor McLaglen

(December 10, 1886 – November 7, 1959)

The tough guy actor with a heart of gold was born on December 10, 1886, in Tunbridge, England. The son of a Protestant Minister, Victor was the second eldest of eight children. After turning eighteen, the adventuresome young man immigrated to Canada. It was there where he found his calling with forays into show business with traveling circuses, vaudeville shows, Wild West extravaganzas, and even prize fighting challenges.

McLaglen's distinguished and award-winning career in motion pictures spanned nearly four decades from 1920 to 1959 and included over 100 films. His early movies found him type cast as the tough guy in action adventure pictures, but as his popularity increased, diversity in roles developed. He was a versatile actor, who was able to move effortlessly between the tough guy, lovable rouge, and debonair leading man; his major film credits include:

- *What Price Glory* (1926)
- *The Magnificent Brute* (1936)
- *Gunga Din* (1939)
- *Fort Apache* (1948)
- *She Wore a Yellow Ribbon* (1949)
- *Rio Grande* (1950)

He was a favorite actor of director John Ford, who cast McLaglen as an Irishmen in many films, even though he was British.

Right:
The 8th Academy Awards Ceremony held on March 5, 1936. From left to right, Irving Thalberg, Bette Davis, Frank Capra, and Victor McLaglen. *Courtesy of the Herald Examiner Collection/ Los Angeles Public Library*

In 1935, McLaglen was nominated and won the Academy Award for best actor for his portrayal of the dim-witted giant in John Ford's *The Informer* and was nominated in 1953 for a best supporting actor Oscar in *The Quiet Man* (1952), co-starring John Wayne.

Victor McLaglen died on November 7, 1959, at his Newport Beach, California, home from congestive heart failure. His funeral service was held at the Church of the Recessional at Forest Lawn, Glendale; in attendance were over 200 mourners that included numerous Hollywood personalities. The eulogy was delivered by fellow actor and good friend, Donald Crisp who spoke of McLaglen as "a great and kindly man of mighty physique and generous nature."

The actor's remains were cremated and are interred in the Columbarium of Eternal Light within the Garden of Memory at Forest Lawn, Glendale. McLaglen is interred only a few feet from legendary actor Humphrey Bogart.

Victor McLaglen's niche in the Columbarium of Eternal Light at Forest Lawn—Glendale.

Bette Davis

(April 5, 1908 – October 6, 1989)

"Hollywood always wanted me to be pretty, but I fought for realism."

"There was more good acting at Hollywood parties than ever appeared on screen."

~Bette Davis

Bette Davis, "The First Lady of the American Screen" was born Ruth Elizabeth Davis on April 5, 1908, in Lowell, Massachusetts. An outgoing child, the young Bette Davis was destined for a career on the stage and film. She studied and excelled in acting under famed drama coach John Murray Anderson. In 1929, Davis made her successful Broadway stage debut in *Broken Promises*. It was in this performance that Hollywood began to take notice of the future award winning actress. In 1930, studio executives at Universal Pictures who offered her a contract and her film debut followed the next year (1931) in *Bad Sister*. The next few pictures that followed were less than successful for Davis and she was dropped by Universal Pictures. Fortunately, Warner Brothers gave her a second chance; she co-starred alongside Academy Award winning actor George Arliss in *The Man Who Played God* (1932). This began what would become a successful eighteen year association with Warner Studios. This relationship was very contentious; she often fought with studio head Jack Warner over top movie roles and even sued the studio in an attempt to break her contact.

Davis' storied film career spanned nearly six decades 1931 to 1989, and included over 120 television and motion picture performances. Her first big smash hit came in 1934's, *Of Human Bondage*, loaned out to RKO Pictures by Warner Studios; Davis cemented her place in Hollywood lore by playing the role of the sullen heroine, Mildred Rogers for which she was nominated for an Academy Award.

During her legendary film career, Davis was nominated for eleven Academy Awards and won twice, her nominated films include:

- *Of Human Bondage* (1934)
- *Dark Victory* (1939)
- *The Letter* (1940)
- *The Little Foxes* (1941)
- *Now, Voyager* (1942)
- *Mr. Skeffington* (1944)
- *All About Eve* (1950)
- *The Star* (1952)
- *What Ever Happened to Baby Jane* (1962)

In 1935, Davis won the first of two best actress Oscars for her portrayal of Joyce Heath in *Dangerous* and won a second award in 1938 in *Jezebel*. During the late 1930s through the mid-1940s, Davis' stature in the film industry grew with every film, but by the end of the decade, her career began to wane and seemed headed for oblivion. A renaissance occurred when she co-starred alongside Anne Baxter in 1950s best picture, *All About Eve*. Her performance in this film is considered by many to be one of the greatest of all time.

During her storied film career, she reigned as one of the most successful and durable stars having clawed and scratched her way to the top the film business. The award-winning actress known for her toughness, huge eyes and haute acting style died on October 6, 1989, in Neuilly, France from breast cancer.

Davis' ornate crypt is found at Forest Lawn Memorial Park, Hollywood Hills, outside of the Court of Remembrance. Her epitaph reads; Bette Davis, April 5, 1908 – October 6, 1989; "She did it the hard way."

Did You Know?

Davis had a very contentious rivalry with fellow actress Joan Crawford and upon hearing the news of her nemesis death was quoted as saying, "You should never say bad things about the dead; you should only say good things... Joan Crawford is dead. Good."

Warner Bros. publicity still of Bette Davis as depicted in her
Academy Award winning performance as Julie in Jezebel (1938).

Right:
Bette Davis' monument at Forest
Lawn—Glendale.

DAVIS

RUTH FAVOR DAVIS
SEPTEMBER 16 1885 – JULY 1, 1961

BARBARA DAVIS BERRY
OCTOBER 25, 1909 – JULY 19, 1979

BETTE DAVIS
APRIL 5, 1908 – OCTOBER 6, 1989

" She did it the hard way "

John Ford

(February 1, 1894 – August 31, 1973)

"How did I get to Hollywood? By train."

~John Ford

John Ford is considered by many to be America's greatest film director, he was born John Martin Feeney on February 1, 1894, in Cape Elizabeth, Maine. He was known as "Pappy" to his closest friends and his storied and award-winning directorial film career spanned nearly five decades from 1917 to 1966 and included 144 motion pictures. The hard-nosed director was best known for his numerous Westerns starring John Wayne, Jimmy Stewart, and Henry Fonda. He is credited with discovering John Wayne and giving him his first big break in motion pictures (*Stagecoach*, 1939). Wayne and Ford made numerous films together and the pair remained very close friends all their lives. Ford's major film credits include:

- *Young Mr. Lincoln* (1939)
- *The Battle of Midway* (1942, he won a best documentary Oscar)
- *They Were Expendable* (1945)
- *Fort Apache* (1948)
- *She Wore a Yellow Ribbon* (1949)
- *Rio Grande* (1950)
- *Mister Roberts* (1955)
- *The Searchers* (1956)
- *The Horse Soldiers* (1959)
- *The Man Who Shot Liberty Valance* (1962)
- *How the West was Won* (1962)

During his legendary film career, Ford was nominated for five best director Academy Awards, winning four times and include:

- *The Informer* (1935, won)
- *Stagecoach* (1939, nominated)
- *The Grapes of Wrath* (1940, won)
- *How Green is My Valley* (1941, won)
- *The Quiet Man* (1952, won)

Did You Know?

Ford was the first director to win back-to-back Oscars in 1941 and 1942. He enlisted in the U.S. Naval reserve in 1934 and retired in 1951 with the honorary rank of rear Admiral.

The award-winning director died on August 31, 1973, at his home in Palm Desert, California, from cancer. His funeral was held at the Blessed Sacrament Catholic Church in Hollywood and in attendance were over 1,400 mourners; counted among them were numerous members of Hollywood's elite. He was eulogized as "the incomparable mater of his trade" by both John Wayne and Cardinal Timothy Manning.

John Ford is buried at Holy Cross Cemetery in Los Angeles, lawn M, lot 304, space 5.

Right:
Director John Ford's grave at Holy Cross Catholic Cemetery.

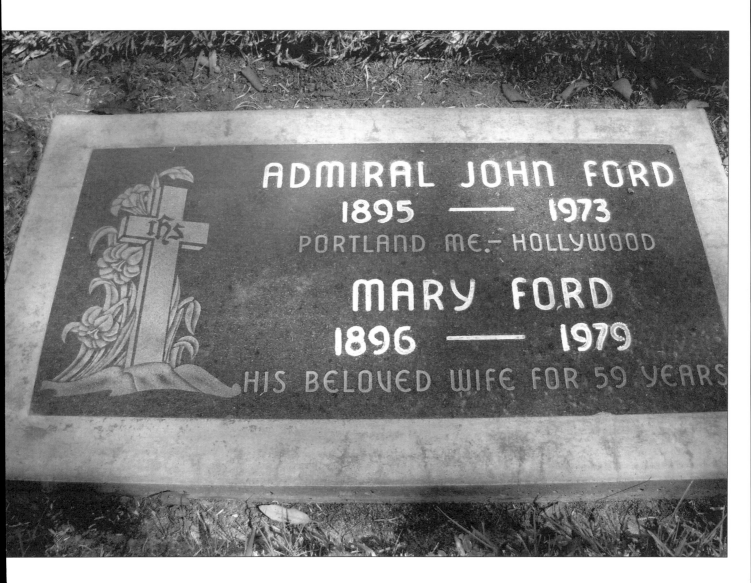

The Ninth Academy Awards Ceremony
"Don't Mess with Bette"

This year's rendition of the annual awards gala was held at the Biltmore Hotel on March 4, 1937, honoring the film industry's best achievements for 1936. Several new award categories were added that included best supporting actor and actress. A committee of fifty industry insiders continued to refine the voting procedures but still shamelessly voted for one another making a mockery of the proceedings. A public outcry for fairness caused the Academy to scrap this procedure and return voting rights back to academy members. The master of ceremony for the evening was actor, comedian, and entertainer, George Jessel. While passing out awards, he was heard to say, "Please keep your thank-yous short, and remember a fellow gave up the British Empire in two minutes." This was in reference to the recent abdication of King Edward VIII of England. Jessel made a huge gaffe, when he presented the best actress award to Luise Rainer. That honor was supposed to go to Bette Davis, the previous year's recipient. A furious Bette Davis found Jessel back stage and berated him on his lack of etiquette. The year's best film went to *The Great Ziegfeld*, a lavish musical, bio-pic, which up until then was the most expensive such film ever produced. This film was a box office success but lacked critical acclaim.

The Nominees and Winners

Best Actor
Gary Cooper, Walter Huston, **Paul Muni**, William Powell, and Spencer Tracy

Best Actress
Irene Dunne, **Luise Rainer**, Carole Lombard, Gladys George, and Norma Shearer

Best Supporting Actor
Mischa Auer, **Walter Brennan**, Stuart Erwin, Basil Rathbone, and Akim Tamiroff

Best Supporting Actress
Bulah Bondi, Alice Brady, Bonita Granville, **Gale Sondergaard**, and Maria Ouspenskaya

Best Director
Frank Capra, George LaCava, Robert Z. Leonard, W.S. Van Dyke, and William Wyler

Paul Muni
(September 22, 1895 – August 25, 1967)

The successful stage and screen actor was born Meshilem Meier Weisenfreund on September 22, 1895, in Lemburg, Austria. His parents were actors who toured small cabarets in Europe and immigrated to the United States in 1902. He and his parents toured small vaudeville theaters throughout the Midwest and by 1926, Muni had graduated to the bright lights of Broadway. In 1928, he signed with 20th Century-Fox studios and it was suggested that he change his name from Weisenfruend to Muni. His first film project, *The Valiant* (1929), was not a box office success but it did earn him a best actor nomination in his first screen appearance.

Muni's award winning film career spanned thirty years (1929-1962) and included twenty-three motion pictures; major film credits include:

- *Scarface* (1929)
- *The Good Earth* (1937)
- *Juarez* (1939)
- *We Are Not Alone* (1939)

Right:
Academy Award winners from 1937; left to right: Paul Muni, Luise Rainer, and Frank Capra. *Courtesy of the Herald Examiner Collection/ Los Angeles Public Library*

He was nominated for six best acting Oscars, winning once; his nominated films were:

- *The Valiant* (1929)
- *I am a Fugitive from a Chain Gang* (1932)
- *Black Fury* (1935)
- *The Life of Emile Zola* (1937)
- *The Last Angry Man* (1959)

...and his only Academy Award win was for portrayal of scientist Louis Pasteur in *The Life of Louis Pasteur* (1936).

In the early 1960s, Muni was tired of the Hollywood life style and retired. He and his wife lived a simple, quiet life in Montecito, California, until August 25, 1967, when the former actor died from a heart attack. Funeral services and burial were held at the Hollywood Memorial Park (now called Hollywood Forever Cemetery).

Muni's unassuming grave is found beneath a cypress tree in the center of the Plains of Abraham lawn (formerly section 14), space 57 at Hollywood Forever Cemetery in Los Angeles, California.

Luise Rainer

(Born January 12, 1910 in Dusseldorf, Germany)

Best actress winner **Luise Rainer** was the first actress to win back-to-back best actress Academy Awards, 1936 and 1937, she is still living and resides in London, England, in a flat previously owned by Vivien Leigh. She outlived all her contemporaries and is currently the oldest living recipient of an Academy Award.

Paul Muni's final resting place at Hollywood Forever Cemetery.

Walter Brennan

(July 25, 1894 – September 21, 1974)

The most successful, recognizable, and dependable character actor of the gold age of cinema, Walter Andrew Brennan, was born July 25, 1894, in Swampscott, Massachusetts. While in college, the young Brennan became interested in acting and traveled the vaudeville circuit performing in small theaters; he also appeared in several films as an extra.

In 1935, he got his big break, appearing in the films, *The Wedding Night* and *The Barbary* Coast, from which he was offered a regular acting contract with MGM studios. Throughout his storied film career, he primarily played the western side kick but was very capable of playing the scoundrel. He was good friends with actor Gary Cooper and co-starred with the iconic actor in numerous films.

Walter Brennan, 1894-1974.

Appearing in over 230 motion picture and television roles from 1925 to 1975, Brennan's most memorable films include:

- *She's Dangerous* (1937)
- *The Adventures of Tom Sawyer* (1938)
- *The Buccaneer* (1938)
- *Meet John Doe* (1941)
- *The Pride of the Yankees* (1942)
- *My Darling Clementine* (1946)
- *Red River* (1948)
- *Tammy and the Bachelor* (1957)
- *Rio Bravo* (1959)

In 1936, Brennan won the first ever supporting actor Oscar for his portrayal of Swan Bostrom in *Come and Get It* (1935). He was nominated for three additional best supporting actor awards and won twice, *Kentucky* (1938, won), *The Westerner* (1940, won), and *Sergeant York* (1941, nominated). Brennan died after a long battle with emphysema on September 21, 1974, at St. John's Hospital in Oxnard, California.

Walter Brennan's final resting place is found at the San Fernando Mission Cemetery, Mission Hills, California in lawn section D, lot 445, space 8.

Gale Sondergaard

(February 15, 1899 – August 14, 1985)

The accomplished stage and film actress was born Edith Holm Sondergaard on February 15, 1899, in Litchfield, Minnesota. She has been described by some as the most talented character actress of her time. From 1935 to 1983, she appeared in over fifty television and motion picture projects that include:

- *The Life of Emile Zola* (1937)
- *Seventh Heaven* (1937)
- *Juarez* (1939)
- *The Cat and the Canary* (1939)
- *The Mark of Zorro* (1940)
- *The Letter* (1940)
- *The Black Cat* (1941)
- *A Night to Remember* (1942)
- *Spider Woman* (1944)

Sondergaard could play the sinister, cunning, and manipulative woman extremely well and was the recipient of the first ever best supporting actress Academy Award in 1936 for her portrayal of Faith Paleologus in *Anthony Adverse* (1935). She was nominated for a second Oscar in 1947 for *Anna and the King of Spain* (1946).

The grave of actor Walter Brennan at the San Fernando Mission Cemetery.

Gale Sondergaard, 1899-1985.

Did You Know?

Sondergaard's look was the inspiration behind the character of the Evil Queen in Disney's *Snow White and Seven Dwarfs* (1937) and she was first offered the part of the Wicked Witch of the West in *The Wizard of Oz* (1939) but refused the role when the character was switched from beautiful to ugly.

In the early 1950s, her director husband Herbert Biberman was singled out as one of the "Hollywood Ten," who were accused of anti-American activities and being involved in the Communist Party by the House Un-American Activities Commission. Sondergaard refused to testify against her husband and was blacklisted. This basically destroyed her successful film career. Eventually, Sondergaard returned to films and television but never achieved the level of fame or success of her early years. She died on August 14, 1985, at the Motion Picture and Television Home in Woodland Hills from a stroke.

Gayle Sondergaard's ashes were scattered at sea by family and friends.

Frank Capra

Best Director winner, Frank Capra's life and career achievements have been discussed earlier in this chapter.

The Tenth Academy Award Ceremony
"It's a Wash Out"

On March 3, 1938, the streets of Los Angeles were flooded and awash from torrents of rain that made movement within the city impossible. The annual awards banquet was cancelled and rescheduled for a week later on March 10, 1938, and was held at the Biltmore Hotel. Unfortunately, due to scheduling conflicts, none of the nominated stars showed up for the ceremony. Even the original host George Jessel backed out because of illness and was replaced by comedian Bob "Bazooka" Burns. The night was filled with stunning upsets and was a turning point in the history of the Academy, when the power of choosing winners switched from the studio heads and stars to the general academy membership. The best picture of the year was no surprise, *The Life of Emile Zola* (1937), a large scale bio-pic that was critically acclaimed and well received by audiences.

The Nominees and Winners

Best Actor
Charles Boyer, **Spencer Tracy**, Fredric March, Robert Montgomery, and Paul Muni

Best Actress
Irene Dunne, Greta Garbo, **Luise Rainer**, Janet Gaynor, and Barbara Stanwyck

Best Supporting Actor
Ralph Bellamy, Thomas Mitchell, **Joseph Schildkraut**, H.B. Warner, and Roland Young

Best Supporting Actress
Alice Brady, Andrea Leeds, Anne Shirley, Claire Trevor, and Dame May Whitty

Best Director
William Dieterle, Sidney Franklin, Gregory LaCava, **Leo McCarey**, and William Wellman

Spencer Tracy

(April 5, 1900 – June 10, 1967)

"Know your lines and don't bump into the furniture."
~Spencer Tracy

One of Hollywood's true legends, Spencer Bonaventure Tracy, was born on April 5, 1900, in Milwaukee, Wisconsin. A boyhood friend of fellow actor Pat O'Brien, Tracy had rugged good looks and boyish mannerisms that made him a successful box office draw for nearly forty years. His legendary career in film started in 1930 and after seventy-eight motion pictures, ended in 1967, just a few months prior to his death.

He was nominated for nine best acting Oscars and was the first male actor to win the award in back to back years, 1937 and 1938. His first Oscar win was for the sea adventure film, *Captains Courageous* (1936), in which he portrayed a light-hearted Portuguese fisherman, who befriends a young stowaway, and his second win was for the bio-pic, *Boy's Town* (1937), in which Tracy portrayed the legendary Father Flanagan. His other Oscar nominated films were:

- *San Francisco* (1936)
- *Father of the Bride* (1951)
- *Bad Day at Black Rock* (1956)
- *Inherit the Wind* (1961)
- *Judgment At Nuremberg* (1962)
- *Guess Who's Coming to Dinner* (1967)

> **Did You Know?**
> Tracy was offered the role of the Penguin in the 1960s television series *Batman* but turned down the role after he was told he could not kill Batman.

Tracy appeared in numerous films with Katharine Hepburn and their on screen chemistry continued off screen. The pair had a twenty plus year romance (of which Hepburn considered him the love her life) but because he was a devout Catholic, he never divorced his wife, actress Louise Treadwell. The couple lived separately for many years and she was aware of and tolerant of Hepburn's love interest in her husband.

A few weeks prior to his death on June 10, 1967, he finished what would be his last motion picture, *Guess Who's Coming to Dinner*, co-starring Katharine Hepburn. The actor had been in failing health for several years and suffered a fatal heart attack at his West Hollywood Hills home.

Right:
Spencer Tracy, 1900-1967.

His private funeral mass was held at the Immaculate Heart Catholic Church attended by nearly 500 close friends, family, and Hollywood dignitaries that included pallbearers Frank Sinatra, Jimmy Stewart, and John Ford. Out of respect for the family, Katharine Hepburn did not attend either the funeral or burial service.

Spencer Tracy is buried at Forest Lawn, Glendale in the private Garden of Everlasting Peace, near the Freedom Mausoleum, and his marker simply reads; "Tracy."

Spencer Tracy's final resting place in the Garden of Everlasting Peace at Forest Lawn—Glendale.

Joseph Schildkraut

(March 22, 1896 – January 21, 1964)

The multi-talented, award-winning actor of stage, screen, and television was born on March 22, 1896, in Vienna, Austria. His American motion picture debut was in 1921 with D.W. Griffith's *Orphan's of the Storm*. His film career would span forty-three years from 1921 to 1964 and included over fifty major motion pictures that include:

- *Viva Villa* (1934)
- *Cleopatra* (1934)
- *Marie Antoinette* (1938)
- *The Three Musketeers* (1939)
- *The Man in the Iron Mask* (1939)
- *The Tell-Tale-Heart* (1941)
- *The Greatest Story Ever Told* (1965)

His strong sturdy voice and exotic good looks allowed for an easy transition from silent films to talkies. In his early films, he tended to play the cunning villain and matinee idol but as his career progressed, he often found himself playing the sweet sympathetic type. Schildkraut won the best supporting actor Oscar in 1938 for his portrayal of Captain Alfred Dreyfus in *The Life of Emile Zola* (1937). His most memorable and moving role was that of Otto Frank, the father of Anne Frank in *The Diary of Anne Frank* (1959).

Only months after marrying his third wife, Leonora Rogers (she was thirty-five years younger than he), the acclaimed actor died from a heart attack at his New York City home. His funeral service was held at the Fairfax Temple in Los Angeles, California, and was attended by over 600 mourners that included many Hollywood personalities.

Joseph Schildkraut's cremated remains are interred at Hollywood Forever Cemetery in the Beth Olam mausoleum, foyer R, niche 212.

Joseph Schildkraut, 1896-1964.

Alice Brady

(November 2, 1892 – October 28, 1939)

One of the cinema's most talented dramatic and comedic actresses of the golden age of film, Mary Rose Brady, was born on November 2, 1892, in New York City. Despite her family connections (she was the daughter of famed Broadway producer William A. Brady). and over her father's strenuous objections (he wanted her to become an opera singer), she pursued a career in the theater and, eventually, motion pictures. Brady's rise to stardom was not easy, despite her family connections. She would appear in seventy-nine motion pictures in a twenty-five year film career (1914 to 1939). Brady had two very distinct stages to her film career, 1914 to 1923; after which she left film to concentrate on a theater career. Then, in 1933, she returned to film, and in a very short productive seven year period, completed twenty-six motion pictures.

Brady was nominated for a best supporting actress Academy Awards in 1937, for her depiction of the comedic, social climbing mother in *My Man Godfrey* (1936), and won the Oscar in 1938 for *In Old Chicago* (1937) in which she portrayed Mrs. Molly O'Leary. Other notable film credits include:

- *Beauty for Sale* (1933)
- *Gold Diggers of 1935* (1935)
- *Let 'em Have It* (1935)
- *Good Bye Broadway* (1938)
- *Young Mr. Lincoln* (1939)

Did You Know?

Brady never actually received her 1938 Oscar; an imposter at the awards ceremony accepted the award on her behalf and walked away with the statuette. Neither the man nor the award was ever seen again and Brady died before the Academy could issue her a replacement.

Brady was prone to hard luck her whole life; in 1930, just as she was about to star in a Broadway play, she suffered a nervous breakdown, and eight years later in 1938, she broke an ankle while performing in another theatrical performance. Tragedy struck the actress for a third and fatal time in 1938, when she was diagnosed with a virulent form of cancer. On October 28, 1939, at the Leroy Sanitarium in New York City, Alice Brady succumbed to the illness, just five days short of her forty-seventh birthday.

Alice Brady, 1892-1939. *Courtesy of the Library of Congress, George G. Bain Collection (LC-DIG-ggbain-31694)*

The gravesite of Alice Brady at Sleepy Hollow Cemetery.

Alice Brady's grave is located in the historic Sleepy Hollow Cemetery, Sleepy Hollow, New York, in the Gibeon 57 section. This is the same cemetery of headless horsemen fame of which Washington Irving wrote about in his famous short story, "The Legend of Sleepy Hollow." The renowned "Headless Horsemen Bridge" is just a short walk from Brady's grave site.

Leo McCarey

(October 3, 1896 – July 5, 1969)

The talented writer, producer, and director Thomas Leo McCarey was born on October 3, 1896, in Los Angeles, California. His foray into motion pictures began as a producer/director for Hal Roach and he is allegedly responsible for putting together the comic duo of Stan Laurel and Oliver Hardy. His directorial film career included 110 motion pictures from 1921 to 1962, and included such classics as:

- *Duck Soup* (1933)
- *Six of a Kind* (1934)
- *The Ruggles of Red Gap* (1935)
- *The Milky Way* (1936)

Director Leo McCarey's final resting place at Holy Cross Catholic Cemetery.

With an easy-going and soft spoken style, McCarey won three Academy Awards, and was nominated for five others in three different categories: best directing, writing, and song. His award winning films include:

- *The Awful Truth* (1937, won best director)
- *Love Affair* (1939, nominated for writing)
- *My Favorite Wife* (1940, nominated for best writing)
- *Going My Way* (1944, won both best director and writing)
- *The Bells of St. Mary's* (1945, nominated for best director)
- *My Son John* (1952, nominated for best writing)
- *An Affair to Remember* (1957, nominated for best original song)

The acclaimed director died on July 5, 1969, at St. John's Hospital in Santa Monica, California, after a lengthy battle with emphysema.

Leo McCarey is buried at Holy Cross Catholic Cemetery, Culver City, California, in section T, tier 44, space 134.

The Eleventh Academy Awards Ceremony
"Hi Ho, Hi Ho, it's Off to Work We Go"

The awards ceremony February 23, 1939, was held for the fifth year in a row at the Biltmore Hotel. The host for the night was Academy Award winning director, Frank Capra. During the evening, Walt Disney received a special award for his animated film, *Snow White and the Seven Dwarfs* (the special Oscar statuette was adorned on the base with seven small Oscars). Spencer Tracy won the best actor Oscar for a second consecutive year and best picture went to the romantic comedy, *You Can't Take It With You*, directed by Frank Capra.

The Nominees and Winners

Best Actor
Charles Boyer, James Cagney, Robert Donat, Leslie Howard, and **Spencer Tracy**

Best Actress
Fay Bainter, **Bette Davis**, Wendy Hiller, Norma Shearer, and Margaret Sullivan

Best Supporting Actor
Walter Brennan, John Garfield, Gene Lockhart, Robert Morley, and Basil Rathbone

Best Supporting Actress
Fay Bainter, Beulah Bondi, Billie Burke, Spring Byington, and Miliza Korius

Best Director
Frank Capra, Michael Curtiz, Norman Taurog, and King Vidor

Spencer Tracy, Bette Davis, Walter Brennan, Frank Capra

Best actor, actress, supporting actor, and director, Spencer Tracy, Bette Davis, Walter Brennan, and Frank Capra have all had their life stories and career achievements discussed earlier in this chapter.

Fay Bainter

(December 7, 1894 – April 16, 1968)

The award winning character actress was born on December 7, 1894, in Los Angeles, California. Her short ten-year film acting career (1934 to 1944) began with *This Side of Heaven* (1934) and concluded with *Dark Waters* (1944). During this brief ten year period, she appeared in twenty-seven motion pictures that included:

- *Quality Street* (1937)
- *The Shinning Hour* (1938)
- *Young Tom Edison* (1940)
- *Woman of the Year* (1942)
- *Cry Havoc* (1943)
- *Heavenly Body* (1944)

In 1939, Bainter was the first actress to be nominated for two separate Academy Awards in the same year, best actress, *White Banners* (1938), and best supporting actress, *Jezebel* (1938). She lost in the best actress category but won the best supporting actress Oscar for her portrayal of Aunt Belle in *Jezebel* (opposite Bette Davis, who won for best actress). Due to confusion in the voting, the Academy was forced to change the rules. Bainter came out of semi-retirement in 1961 to film, *The Children's Hour*, and was again honored with a best supporting actress Oscar nomination but lost to Rita Moreno. Bainter died on April 16, 1968 at her home in Los Angeles, California, from pneumonia. Her funeral service was held at the All Saints Episcopal Church in Beverly Hills.

Fay Bainter is interred at Arlington National Cemetery, Washington D.C., lawn section 3, space 2456-1, next to her husband, U.S. Navy, Lt. Commander Reginald Venable.

The grave site of Fay Bainter at Arlington National Cemetery.

Chapter Three

1939

The Greatest Year in Film and
The Twelfth Academy Awards Ceremony

It was a window into cinematic time as Hollywood gathered to celebrate itself on a brisk and clear night on February 29, 1940, at the Twelfth Annual Academy Awards. Returning to the Ambassador Hotels, Cocoanut Grove Ballroom after a nine year hiatus, the ceremony was hosted for the first time by actor and comedian, Bob Hope (he would go on to host or co-host the awards show a record seventeen times). Those that gathered that night did not realize that they were standing on the mountain top and that this year would be the summit of Hollywood's golden age.

What made this year so special? It was a watershed moment in cinematic history, with the studio system at its height, but big changes were on the horizon. The political situation in Europe was beginning to affect America and Hollywood. There was a sense that something horrible was about to happen. Many changes were impacting Hollywood. The Great Depression had hit. There were technical innovations in sound recording. Technicolor arrived and every department of the studios was at peak performance. This produced films that are still remembered today. It was a year when every studio went all out; everything was on a bigger canvas.

This year each major studio produced an extraordinary number of legendary films. MGM produced films such as *Ninotchka*, starring Greta Garbo in comedic role that satirized Russia's Communist system. It was billed as "Garbo laughs," an attempt by the studio to make her more appealing to the mass audiences. This was one of Garbo's last great movies before her self-imposed exile from Hollywood. This same year saw MGM undertake one of the most ambitious and innovative films in movie history…the live action musical, *The Wizard of Oz*. This American fairy tale that would utilize a new form of film making technique called "Technicolor," that would bring fantasy to life in amazing colors that would thrill audiences for decades to come. The film would also make an instant star out of a virtually unknown actress, Judy Garland. Another MGM film classic

from 1939 was *The Women*, which was a unique movie about independent women that featured an all female cast, including Joan Crawford, Norma Shearer, and Rosalind Russell. This year also produced *Good Bye, Mr. Chips*, starring Robert Donat and Greer Garson.

Warner studios produced films with excitement and attitude. Their contribution to 1939 included what became known as the summit of the crime films, *The Roaring 20's*, starring James Cagney and Humphrey Bogart, the western epic, *Dodge City*, starring Errol Flynn and Olivia de Havilland, *The Private Lives of Elizabeth and Essex*, *Juarez*, and *Dark Victory*, all starred the independent and domineering Bette Davis, who was seen as a force of nature on and off the screen. Other notable Warner studio releases included the politically controversial *Confessions of a Nazi Spy*.

While Paramount pictures produced *Midnight*, starring Claudette Colbert, and the Cecile B. DeMille epic *Union Pacific*, Universal Pictures, known for its classic monster movies, released *Son of Frankenstein*, starring both Boris Karloff and Bela Lugosi and released *Destry Rides Again* with James Stewart. Columbia pictures released Frank Capra's classic, *Mr. Smith Goes to Washington*, starring James Stewart. RKO pictures released *Gunga Din* starring Cary Grant and Douglas Fairbanks, Jr., *The Hunchback of Notre Dame* starring Charles Laughton and Maureen O'Hara, *The Story of Verne and Irene Castle*, the last Fred Astaire and Ginger Rogers dance film, and *Love Affair*, starring Irene Dunn. A newcomer to the film business, 20th Century Fox, produced *Jesse James* with Tyrone Power, and three films by legendary film director John Ford, *Drums Along the Mohawk*, *Young Mr. Lincoln*, and *Stage Coach* which starred another virtually unknown actor John Wayne. United Artists released *Of Mice and Men* and *Wuthering Heights*, starring Laurence Olivier.

But the biggest box office success of 1939 and perhaps the greatest film ever made, *Gone with the Wind*, was released by Selznick International Pictures. The film was a landmark, challenging records for run time, budget, size, and censorship. It was a massive undertaking, taking longer to make than any other movie. At the time, it was the biggest box office hit in Hollywood history. It was a record that would set the standard for decades to come and in a year of extra ordinary cinematic achievement...*Gone With the Wind* would represent the pinnacle of the Hollywood studio system. And like the old South, Hollywood would never again rise so high as in 1939.

This year the Academy of Motion Picture Arts and Sciences allowed ten films to be nominated for best picture; *Dark Victory, Gone With the Wind, Good Bye, Mr. Chips, Love Affair, Mr. Smith Goes to Washington, Ninotchka, Of Mice and Men, Stagecoach, The Wizard of Oz,* and *Wuthering Heights.* The big winner for night would be Victor Fleming's Civil War epic motion picture, *Gone With the Wind.* This film would receive a record twelve Oscar nominations and would win eight awards, including best picture. All the top awards with the exception of best actor, and supporting actor went to this film. Newcomer, actress Judy Garland received a pint-sized, honorary Oscar for her outstanding juvenile performance as Dorothy in MGM's, *The Wizard of Oz.*

Nominees and Winners

Best Actor
Robert Donat, Clark Gable, Laurence Olivier, Mickey Rooney, and James Stewart

Best Actress
Bette Davis, **Vivien Leigh**, Irene Dunne, Greta Garbo, and Greer Garson

Best Supporting Actor
Brian Aherne, Harry Carey, Brian Donlevy, **Thomas Mitchell**, and Claude Rains

Best Supporting Actress
Olivia de Havilland, Geraldine Fitzgerald, **Hattie McDaniel**, Edna May Oliver, and Maria Ouspenskaya

Best Director
Frank Capra, **Victor Fleming**, John Ford, Sam Wood, and William Wyler

Group portrait of the cast of crew of the film, *Gone With the Wind*; left to right, clockwise: Clark Gable; Eric Stacey (Asst. Director); Walter Plunkett (Costumes); Unknown; George Culkor (Director); Lee Garmes (Camera); Unknown; Unknown; James Potevin (Chief Electrician); Unknown; Center: Vivien Leigh. They are filming the Paris hat sequence. *Courtesy of the Los Angeles Public Library*

Robert Donat

(March 18, 1905 – June 9, 1958)

This gifted but reserved actor of both screen and theater was born Friedrich Robert Donath, March 18, 1905, in Withington, England. His career in motion pictures lasted twenty-six years (1932-1958) in which he made only twenty films. He was very finicky about the roles he chose and was not fond of the "Hollywood scene," thus the majority of his pictures were filmed in his native Britain. His notable film credits include:

- *The Private Lives of Henry VIII* (1933)
- *The Count of Monte Cristo* (1934)
- *The 39 Steps* (1935)
- *The Cure for Love* (1950)
- *The Lease of Life* (1954)

He was nominated for a best acting Oscar in 1939 for *The Citadel* (1938) and won the award the following year 1940, for his portrayal of Mr. Chips in MGM's *Goodbye, Mr. Chips* (1939).

The actor suffered from severe asthma and other illnesses most of his life and died suddenly on June 9, 1958. He had just finished the film, *The Inn of the Sixth Happiness* (1958) a few weeks earlier, when he collapsed and was taken to a local London area hospital. At first it was thought that Donat had died from an acute attack of asthma but after an autopsy, the cause of death was changed to cerebral thrombosis caused by an undiagnosed brain tumor.

His poignant and prophetic last words on screen were said to co-star Ingrid Bergman's character, "Stay here...for a little. It will comfort me as I leave, to know it. We shall never see each other again, I think, Farewell." Bergman said later that she felt intuitively, that something was wrong with Donat and that her tearfulness was not acting but real in the film's final scene.

Robert Donat's remains were cremated and his ashes scattered in section 8 of the East Fincheley Cemetery (formerly known as Saint Marylebonne) in East Finchely, England.

Did You Know?

Robert Donat was offered and declined the lead role in the 1935 film, *Captain Blood;* this left an opening for an unknown actor and launched the career of the legendary Errol Flynn.

Robert Donat, 1905-1958.

Vivien Leigh

(November 5, 1913 – July 7, 1967)

"I'm not a film star, I am an actress. Being a film star is such a false life, lived for fake values and for publicity."

~Vivien Leigh

The two-time Academy Award winning actress was born Vivian Mary Hartley in Darjeeling, India, a city near the foot of Mount Everest. Her father Ernest Hartley was a Calcutta stock broker. She began her career on the stage in her early teens and in 1935 appeared on the London stage for the first time. She changed her stage name to Vivien Leigh because it sounded more feminine, using her first husband's (Herbert Leigh Holman) middle name as her new last name and changed the "a" in Vivian to an "e."

Leigh was known for her fiery personality on and off screen and in a short twenty-year film career (1935 to 1965), appeared in nineteen films that included:

- *Things are Looking Up* (1935)
- *Gentlemen's Agreement* (1935)
- *Fire Over London* (1937)
- *Waterloo Bridge* (1940)
- *Caesar and Cleopatra* (1945)
- *Anna Karenina* (1948)
- *The Deep Blue Sea* (1955)
- *Ship of Fools* (1965)

Leigh is best known for her famous portrayal of firebrand heroine Scarlett O'Hara in Victor Flemings Civil War epic, *Gone with the Wind* (1939). This performance starring opposite Clark Gable earned her the first of two best actress Academy Awards (1940). Her second best actress Oscar (1952) came in *A Street Car Named Desire* (1951) in which she portrayed the neurotic Blance DuBois starring opposite Marlon Brando. After 1951, her film career began to wane, and she appeared more on the stage.

Did You Know?

Leigh was married to fellow stage and screen legend Laurence Olivier from 1940 to 1960 and he is credited with suggesting to David O. Selznick that she play the role of Scarlett O' Hara.

Right:
Vivien Leigh.

The celebrated actress was beleaguered with illness most of her adult life; she suffered from manic depressive episodes (bipolar disorder), endured the tragedy of two miscarriages, one of which occurred as the result of an onset accident while filming *Caesar and Cleopatra* (1944), and she contracted tuberculosis in her early thirties. On July 7, 1967, while at her London apartment, Leigh died from the tuberculosis that had plagued most of her adult life. Following her death and as a tribute to the award winning actress, the lights of the West London theater district were dimmed in her honor.

Leigh's ashes are scattered near her country home on the Lake at Tickerage Mill, East Sussex, England.

Thomas Mitchell

(July 11, 1892 – December 17, 1962)

Known as one of Hollywood's greatest character actors, Thomas Mitchell was born on July 11, 1892, in Elizabeth, New Jersey. The heavyset character actor of Irish descent is best known for his portrayal of Gerald O'Hara, the father of Scarlett O'Hara in *Gone with the Wind* (1939). In a show business career that spanned nearly four decades, 1923-1961, he appeared in fifty-seven motion pictures and numerous television programs that include:

* *Lost Horizon* (1937)
* *Man of the People* (1937)
* *Mr. Smith Goes to Washington* (1939)
* *The Hunchback of Notre Dame* (1939)
* *Dark Waters* (1944)
* *High Noon* (1952)

Other famous films in which he appeared are *It's a Wonderful Life* (1946), starring Jimmy Stewart, in which Mitchell portrayed the absent minded, Uncle Billy, and his last film *A Pocket Full of Miracles* (1961), which starred Bette Davis and Glenn Ford. During his long and successful film career, Mitchell was twice nominated for a best supporting actor Oscar, for the role of Dr. Kersaint in *The Hurricane* (1937) and won the award for his portrayal of Doc Boone in *Stage Coach* (1939).

Mitchell was the first actor to win the Triple Crown of acting, best supporting actor Academy Award for *Stage Coach* (1939), a Tony Award in 1953 for *Hazel Flagg*, and an Emmy for best actor in 1953. On December 17, 1962, Mitchell died at his Beverly Hills home after a long struggle with bone cancer. His funeral service was private and held at his home with only family members and a few close friends in attendance.

Thomas Mitchell's remains were cremated and it is alleged that his ashes are held in storage at the Chapel of the Pines Crematory in Los Angeles, California.

Hattie McDaniel

(June 10, 1892 – October 26, 1952)

The first African-American to win an Academy Award was born in Wichita, Kansas. She began her career in show business in the 1910s as a band vocalist, continued into radio, then into film and television. Her award-winning film career produced ninety-five motion pictures from 1932 to 1949. She is primarily known for playing house servant roles and is perhaps best recognized as Mammy—the housekeeper in *Gone with the Wind* (1939). It was for this role that she won the best supporting actress Oscar in 1940. Her other notable films include:

* *The Golden West* (1932)
* *Judge Priest* (1934)
* *The Little Colonel* (1935)
* *Show Boat* (1936)
* *The Mad Miss Manton* (1938)
* *The Shining Hour* (1938)
* *Song of the South* (1946)

McDaniel died on October 26, 1952, at the Motion Picture and Television County Home in Woodland, Hills, California, after a long battle with breast cancer. Her funeral service was held at the Independent Church of Christ in Los Angeles where numerous Hollywood dignitaries were in attendance. Outside the church thousands of people waited to pay their last respects to the famed actress.

Right:
Hattie McDaniels gravesite at
Angeles Rosedale Cemetery.

It was McDaniel's express final wish to be buried at Hollywood Forever Cemetery, but she was denied such a request due to racial bias at the time. Instead she was interred at Angelus Rosedale Cemetery in Los Angeles. Her unassuming grave is located near the front entrance to the cemetery. On the forty-seventh anniversary of her death, October 26, 1999, a memorial cenotaph marker was placed at Hollywood Forever Cemetery by relatives, partially fulfilling her final wish.

Hattie McDaniels memorial cenotaph at Hollywood Forever Cemetery.

Victor Fleming

(February 23, 1889 – January 6, 1949)

The acclaimed film director was born on February 23, 1889, in Pasadena, California. He began his career in Hollywood as a stuntman but soon found that his true calling was behind the camera as a director. Fleming's motion picture directorial career spanned nearly thirty years from 1919 to 1948, and included forty-eight films. He won the 1940 best director Oscar for *Gone with the Wind* and is also famous for directing *The Wizard of Oz* (1939). Other notable film credits include:

- *The Way of All Flesh* (1927)
- *The Virginian* (1929)
- *Renegades* (1930)
- *Treasure Island* (1934)
- *Captains Courageous* (1937)
- *Dr. Jekyll and Mr. Hyde* (1941)
- *Joan of Arc* (1948)

On January 6, 1949, while vacationing with his family near Cottonwood, Arizona, the award-winning director died of a heart attack. His funeral was held at the Alban's Episcopal Church in West Los Angeles. In attendance were numerous celebrities including Jimmy Stewart, John Wayne, Louis B. Mayer, Samuel Goldwyn, and Van Johnson.

Fleming is interred at Hollywood Forever in the Abbey of the Psalms, Sanctuary of Refuge in crypt 2081.

Did You Know?
Victor Fleming is the only director to have two films in the top ten of the American Film Institute's list of the 100 greatest American films of all time, *Gone with the Wind* #4 and *The Wizard of Oz* #6.

Director Victor Fleming's crypt at Hollywood Forever Cemetery.

Judy Garland

(June 10, 1922 – June 22, 1969)

"I was born at the age of 12 on a MGM lot."

"It's lonely and cold at the top…lonely and cold."
~Judy Garland

The sweet and innocent child star of numerous legendary MGM musicals of the golden age of cinema was born Frances Ethel Gumm on June 10, 1922, in Grand Rapids, Minnesota. The youngest daughter of vaudeville performers Frank and Ethel Gumm, young Frances joined the family business at the age of two, performing song and dance routines with her two older sisters. Most of her childhood was spent on the road and this and other factors would lead to trauma and heartache later in life.

In 1935, at the age of thirteen, young Frances was discovered by MGM studio head Louis B. Mayer. She changed her name to Judy Garland, a hybrid of the popular song "Judy" and "Garland" after the famous movie critic, Robert Garland. Judy Garland's career began, but early successes were far and few between. Her film debut was in 1936's *Pigskin Parade*, but it wasn't until three years later that she would rocket to super stardom.

The year 1939 would be a watershed year for Garland. MGM finally cast her in a movie that could showcase her talents, *The Wizard of Oz* (1939). In this film, Garland portrayed Dorothy, an orphan living with her aunt and uncle in Kansas. She gets whisked away by a twister to the land of Oz, on the other side of the rainbow. Her sweet and poignant performance and delivery of the song "Somewhere Over the Rainbow" helped earn Judy a special best juvenile performance Academy Award. This performance would propel Garland into legendary status.

In a film career that would span three decades (1936-1969), Garland would appear in over forty feature motion pictures that include:

- *Broadway Melody of 1938* (1938)
- *Strike Up the Band* (1940)
- *Babes on Broadway* (1941)
- *For Me and My Gal* (1942)
- *Meet Me in St. Louis* (1944)
- *The Ziegfeld Follies* (1945)
- *Easter Parade* (1948)
- *A Star is Born* (1954)

She also appeared alongside actor Mickey Rooney in numerous films such as:

- *Love Finds Andy Hardy* (1938)
- *Andy Hardy Meets Debutante* (1940)
- *Life Begins for Andy Hardy* (1941)

She was nominated for two best actress Oscars, *A Star is Born* (1954) and *Judgment at Nuremberg* (1961).

Groucho Marx, legendary actor and comedian commented on Garland's not winning the 1955 best actress Oscar for *A Star is Born*, "as the biggest robbery since the Brink's heist."

Right:
Judy Garland, 1922-1969.

Did You Know?
Garland is the mother of actresses Liza Minnelli and Lorna Luft. Daughter Liza was once married to Jack Haley, Jr., the son of Jack Haley, who played the tin man in the *Wizard of Oz*. Garland is also a first cousin twice removed of U.S. President and Civil War hero, Ulysses S. Grant.

While Garland's film career was a success, her personal life was a wreck. At an early age she developed a drug problem related to weight issues. She would have numerous affairs with many of her acting co-stars, such as Frank Sinatra and James Mason. Of her five marriages, four would end in divorce. Her battle with drugs and alcohol would be front-page tabloid news most of her adult life. On the evening of June 22, 1969, Garland was found dead in the bathroom of her rented Chelsea, London apartment from an accidental overdose of barbiturates. Her funeral was held at the Frank E. Campbell funeral chapel in Manhattan, New York. An estimated 20,000 well wishers paid their final respects to the legendary actress. Actor James Mason delivered the eulogy. At the funeral, *Wizard of Oz* co-star Ray Bolger commented, "She [Judy] just plain wore out." Controversy erupted after the funeral as to who was going to pay the expenses. As a result, Garland's body lay in a temporary crypt for over a year until her daughter, Liza Minnelli, raised enough funds to have her mother properly buried.

Judy Garland's final resting place is found at Ferncliff Cemetery in Hartsdale, New York, in the main mausoleum, unit 9, alcove HH, crypt 31.

Judy Garland's final resting place at Ferncliff Cemetery.

Technical Awards for 1939

Hal C. Kern

(July 14, 1894 – February 24, 1985)

James E. Newcom

(Unknown)

Hal C. Kern and James E. Newcom won the award for film editing on *Gone with the Wind*. Kern is interred at Forest Lawn Glendale in the Great Mausoleum, columbarium of Unity, niche 11989. James E. Newcom's burial location is unknown.

Robert L. Wheeler

(February 5, 1905 – January 10, 1990)

The Oscar for best art direction went to Robert L. Wheeler, *Gone with the* Wind, and he is interred at the Chapel of the Pines, Los Angeles, Deodora Hall South, section U, niche 68.

Harold Arlen

(February 15, 1905 – April 23, 1986)

E.Y. Harburg

(April 8, 1898 – March 5, 1981)

Best song went to *Over the Rainbow*, music by Harold Arlen and lyrics by E.Y. Harburg. Arlen is buried at Ferncliff Cemetery, Hartsdale, New York, Hickory lawn, space 1666 and Harburg's ashes are scattered at an unknown location.

Herbert Stothart

(September 11, 1885 – February 1, 1949)

The award for best original score went to Herbert Stothart for *The Wizard of Oz*; he is interred at Forest Lawn Glendale, Everlasting love lawn, lot 982.

Sidney Howard

(June 26, 1891 – August 23, 1939)

The best original screen play went to Sidney Howard for *Gone with the Wind*; he is buried at Tyringham Cemetery, Tyringham, Massachusetts.

Gregg Toland

(May 29, 1904 – September 26, 1948)

Ernest Hailer

(Unknown)

Ray Rennahan

(May 1, 1896 – May 19, 1908)

The Oscar's for best cinematography black and white went to **Gregg Toland** for *Wuthering Heights* and for best color cinematography **Ernest Hailer** and **Ray Rennahan** for *Gone with the Wind*. Toland's cremated remains are interred at Hollywood Forever Cemetery in the Chapel Colonade, lower floor, Hailer's burial location is unknown, and Rennahan is interred at Forest Lawn Hollywood Hills in the Abiding love lawn, lot 4772, space 4.

Lyle R. Wheeler

(February 2, 1905 – January 10, 1990)

Best Art Direction – *Gone with the Wind*. His ashes are interred at the Chapel of the Pines, Deodora hall South, niche 68.

Lewis R. Foster

(August 5, 1898 – June 10, 1974)

Best Story – *Mr. Smith Goes to Washington*. He is buried at Forest Lawn Glendale, Whispering Pines, L-810, space 7.

Fred Sersen

(February 24, 1890 – December 11, 1962)

E. H. Hansen

(1870-1947)

Best Visual Effects – *The Rain Came*. Sersen's ashes are interred at Forest Lawn Glendale, Garden of Memory, Columbarium of Eternal Light, niche 548 and Hansen is buried at Hollywood Forever Memorial Park, Garden of Legends, section 8.

Chapter Four
The Award Winners of the 1940's

The first half of the decade was dominated by the cataclysm of World War II, the consequences of which lingered for decades, after which the world view changed with the divergent ideologies of the West and that of Communism. The Great Depression was at an end; the war had brought jobs and kick started the sputtering economy. A new national pride and patriotism developed. Long gone were the days of free spending, freewheeling, and do-as-you-want attitudes of the 1920s, but also gone were the depressed attitudes of the 1930s. The 1940s were a time of cautious optimism and the rise of conservative values.

During this decade, Hollywood evolved and muted its extravagance with award ceremonies that reflected the changes in national attitude. The achievements of American cinematic endeavors brought about some of the greatest films of all-time; *Citizen Kane* (1941), *The Maltese Falcon* (1941), *Casablanca* (1942), and *It's a Wonderful Life* (1946), just to name a few. This decade also saw the rise of screen personalities, stars such as Jimmy Stewart, Humphrey Bogart, James Cagney, Ingrid Bergman, and Joan Crawford.

The Thirteenth Academy Awards Ceremony
"A Fireside Chat"

The award gala was held on February 27, 1941, at the Biltmore Hotel and the master of ceremonies was award-winning film producer and Academy President, Walter Wanger. For the first time in the short history of the awards banquet, the winners were not leaked to the press beforehand. Instead, the results were officially sealed and held by Price-Waterhouse until announced at the event. President Franklin Roosevelt became the first President to address the event via a live radio broadcast from the White House. In his address, he praised the film industry for its charitable work and for its promoting of "the American way of life." There were no clear cut favorites in any of the major award categories and the best picture of the year went to Alfred Hitchcock's psychological thriller, *Rebecca*.

The Nominees and Winners

Best Actor
Charlie Chaplan, Henry Fonda, **James Stewart**, Raymond Massey, and Laurence Olivier

Best Actress
Bette Davis, Joan Fontaine, Katharine Hepburn, **Ginger Rogers**, Martha Scott

Best Supporting Actor
Albert Bassermann, **Walter Brennan**, William Gargan, Jack Oakie, and James Stephenson

Best Supporting Actress
Judith Anderson, **Jane Darwell**, Ruth Hussey, Barbara O'Neil, and Marjorie Rambeau

Best Director
George Cukor, **John Ford**, Alfred Hitchcock, Sam Wood, and William Wyler

James Stewart
(May 20, 1908 – July 2, 1997)

"Never treat your audiences as customers, always as partners."

~Jimmy Stewart

A true Hollywood icon who was known as the "everyman" of American cinema, was born James Maitland Stewart on May 20, 1908, in Indiana, Pennsylvania. He began his career in show business on the stage. After a less than spectacular beginning, Stewart got his big break at MGM studios, when a talent scout for the studio saw him perform and offered him a role in *The Murder Man* (1935) starring Spencer Tracy. From 1935 to 1992 he appeared in over eighty motion pictures. He had a great range as an actor but in his early career primarily played the role of the soft spoken and honest person. Later on he took on roles that portrayed tough and cynical characters.

During World War II, Stewart enlisted in the Army Air Corp and flew twenty-five bombing missions over Germany and attained the rank of full Colonel by the end of the war. For his gallantry and service, he was awarded the Croix de Guerre from France and several U.S. Army Air Medals with clusters. After the war, he returned to Hollywood and resumed is film career.

During his long and illustrious motion picture career, he was the favorite actor of numerous legendary directors including Frank Capra, John Ford, and Alfred Hitchcock. The films they made together would become some of Hollywood's all-time classics. Stewart's most notable film credits include:

- *Wife vs. Secretary* (1936)
- *Vivacious Lady* (1938)
- *Call Northside 777* (1948)
- *The Stratton Story* (1949)
- *The Glenn Miller Story* (1954)
- *Rear Window* (1954)
- *The Spirit of St. Louis* (1957)
- *Vertigo* (1958)
- *How the West was Won* (1962)
- *The Flight of the Phoenix* (1965)
- *The Shootist* (1976)
- *Airport '77* (1977)

Did You Know?
Stewart's best acting Oscar statuette from 1940 has the word "Philadelphia" misspelled and after the ceremony gave it to his father for display in the family hardware store in Indiana, Pennsylvania, where it remained for twenty-five years.

James Stewart, circa 1934. *Courtesy of the Library of Congress, Carl Van Vechten Collection (LC-USZ62-103682)*

Jimmy Stewarts grave at Forest Lawn—Glendale.

Stewart won his first and only best actor Oscar in 1941, for his portrayal of Macaulay Connor, a tabloid reporter with distrust for the wealthy in *The Philadelphia Story* (1940). He was nominated for four additional best acting Academy Awards, *Mr. Smith Goes to Washington* (1939), *It's a Wonderful Life* (1946), *Harvey* (1950), and *Anatomy of a Murder* (1959). He was the recipient of a lifetime achievement Academy Award in 1985 for his fifty years of memorable performances and high ideals on and off the screen.

After the death of his wife, Gloria, in 1994, Stewart rarely made public appearances and basically secluded himself in his Beverly Hills home. On July 2, 1997, he died from cardiac arrest and pulmonary embolism following respiratory issues. Stewart had been in ill health for several years prior to his death. His funeral service at the Beverly Hills Church attracted hundreds of mourners including numerous Hollywood celebrities.

Jimmy Stewart is buried at Forest Lawn Memorial Park in Glendale, California, in the Wee Kirk Churchyard, lot 8, space 2.

Ginger Rogers

(July 16, 1911 – April 25, 1996)

"The biggest reason a celebrity loses his old friends is that unless they become celebrities too, they can't compete with you spending-wise. Even the few who wish to try."

~Ginger Rogers

The award-winning actress, comedian, and dancer was born Virginia Katherine McMath in Independence, Missouri. Her parents divorced when she was a young child and Rogers was raised primarily by her mother, Lela. Her road to show business began as a dancer in her teens, when she won a 1925 Charleston contest, from which she was offered a regular role in a touring vaudeville company. In 1929, she discovered the acting bug and made her Broadway stage debut in *Top Speed*. Success on the stage caused Hollywood to take notice, and Rogers' iconic career on the silver screen began with 1930's *Young Man of Manhattan*. Her film career spanned five decades (1930-1983), in which she appeared in seventy-three feature motion pictures. She is best known for the ten films in which she co-starred with Fred Astaire. Their effortless teamwork on the dance floor and debonair style became a trademark in numerous films of the 1930s such as:

- *Flying Down to Rio* (1933)
- *The Gay Divorcee* (1934)

- *Top Hat* (1935)
- *Roberta* (1935)
- *Swing Time* (1936)
- *Shall We Dance* (1937)
- *Carefree* (1938)

Did You Know?
Rogers was not a classically trained dancer and was a devout Christian Scientist, who boasted that she never drank alcohol or smoked.

She won her first and only best actress Academy Award in 1941 for the dramatic portrayal of a white-collar working girl from the wrong side of the tracks, Kitty Foyle in *Kitty Foyle: The Natural History of a Woman* (1940). Rogers other notable film credits include:

- *42nd Street* (1933)
- *Vivacious Lady* (1938)

Ginger Rogers and Fred Astaire mid-1930s.
Courtesy of the Los Angeles Public Library

- *Bachelor Mother* (1939)
- *Tom, Dick, and Harry* (1941)
- *I'll Be Seeing You* (1944)
- *Monkey Business* (1952)

She made her last on screen performance in the 1965 film, *Harlow*, after which she appeared exclusively on stage and television.

On April 25, 1996, Ginger Rogers died from congestive heart failure at her home in Rancho Mirage, California. She had suffered from poor health for several years preceding her death, tormented by several strokes that left her wheel chair bound.

Ginger Rogers is buried at Oakwood Memorial Park in Chatsworth, California, next to her beloved mother in the Vale of Memory lawn E, lot 303, space 1. She ironically rests for eternity just a short distance from her most famous on screen partner, Fred Astaire (Sequoia lawn G, lot 82, space 4).

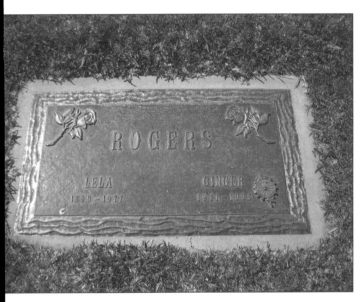

Ginger Rogers final resting place at Oakwood Memorial Park.

Jane Darwell

(October 15, 1879 – August 13, 1967)

Typecast as the matronly grandmother type for most of her film career, the award-winning actress of stage and film was born Mary "Patti" Woodward on October 15, 1879, in Palmyra, Missouri. Her father a high-level railroad executive disapproved of initial foray into show business as a mezzo-soprano opera singer. Not wanting to offend him or the family, she changed her name. Her true calling came late, when

in 1912, at the age of thirty-three, Darwell made her stage acting debut. A year later, she began a successful motion picture career that would span five decades (1913-1964), that included nearly 200 film and television appearances. Darwell won the Academy Award for best supporting actress in 1941 for her portrayal of Ma Joad in *The Grapes of Wrath* (1940).

Darwell was able to make a smooth transition from silent films to talking pictures because of her versatility as a character actress, notable film credits include:

- *Tom Sawyer* (1930)
- *Curly Top* (1935)
- *The Zero Hour* (1939)
- *Gone with the Wind* (1939)
- *My Darling Clementine* (1946)
- *Three Godfathers* (1948)

In 1964, she appeared in her final motion picture. Walt Disney personally persuaded her to come out of retirement to play the memorable role of "the bird woman" in *Mary Poppins*. Jane Darwell died at age eighty-seven on August 13, 1967, from a heart attack at the Motion Picture Country Home and Hospital in Woodland Hills, California.

Jane Darwell is buried at Forest Lawn Memorial Park, Glendale, in the Whispering Pines lawn, lot 1817. Her unassuming grave is adorned with both her given (Patti Woodward) and screen names (Jane Darwell).

Jane Darwell's burial plot at Forest Lawn—Glendale.

Walter Brennan, John Ford

The lives and film accomplishments of best supporting actor Walter Brennan and best director John Ford are discussed in chapter two.

The Fourteenth Academy Awards Ceremony
"Sibling Rivalry"

On February 26, 1942, two months following the surprise attack on Pearl Harbor and America's entry into World War II, a jittery Fourteenth Academy Awards banquet was held. For a second year in a row (and seventh time overall) the event took place at the Biltmore Hotel in Los Angeles. The host for the evening was Bob Hope, who (with the help of fellow comedian Jack Benny) brought some much needed levity to the otherwise toned-down affair.

Best actress nominee, Bette Davis, boycotted the event because the Academy board of directors would not acquiesce to her demands that the event be held in a theater with the public being allowed to purchase tickets. Newcomer, Orson Wells, also did not attend the banquet and his name was heartily booed by the audience, when it was announced that he had won for best screen play (*Citizen Kane*). Wells' recent negative comments against the studio system seemed to have ruffled a few feathers.

Throughout the evening, suspense built as to which feuding sister would win best actress honors, Olivia de Havilland or Joan Fontaine, and which film, *How Green Was My Valley* or *Citizen Kane*, would take home the best picture Oscar. *How Green Was My Valley* would take the honors as 1941's best film but it would be *Citizen* Kane, which would go on to be considered (by many) the greatest motion picture of all-time. It is ironic that this film (*Citizen Kane*) would astoundingly only win one category (best original screen play). Also nominated for a best picture Oscar this year was the legendary film classic, *The Maltese Falcon* (1941), starring Humphrey Bogart and Peter Lorre.

The Nominees and Winners

Best Actor
Cary Grant, **Gary Cooper**, Walter Huston, Roger Montgomery, and Orson Wells

Best Actress
Bette Davis, Olivia de Havilland, **Joan Fontaine**, Greer Garson, and Barbara Stanwyck

Best Supporting Actor
Walter Brennan, Charles Colburn, **Donald Crisp**, James Gleason, and Sydney Greenstreet

Best Supporting Actress
Sara Allgood, **Mary Astor**, Patricia Collinge, Teresa Wright, and Margaret Wycherly

Best Director
John Ford, Alexander Hall, Howard Hawks, Orson Welles, and William Wyler

Gary Cooper
(May 7, 1901 – May 13, 1961)

"In Westerns you were permitted to kiss your horse but never your girl."

~Gary Cooper

The legendary leading man who was known for his strong silent type characters was born Frank James Cooper on May 7, 1901, in Helena, Montana. The son of a Montana State Supreme Court Justice, Cooper was a true "Westerner," and was raised and worked on the family ranch. Prior to becoming an actor, Cooper aspired to be an artist, attending Grinnell College in Iowa. By the early 1920s, Cooper was in Los Angles, where he worked in numerous films as an extra and stuntman. It was Nan Collins, an agent and casting director at United Artists Studios that suggested he change his name to Gary Cooper. His big break came in 1926, when MGM cast him in *The Winning of Barbara Worth*, co-starring Ronald Colman. This film got the attention of Paramount Studios, who quickly signed him to a long-term contract. Cooper was now on a path to super stardom. In a film career that spanned nearly four decades (1923-1961), he appeared in over 110 motion pictures and portrayed some of the most memorable characters in motion picture history. His film credits include:

Right:
Gary Cooper, 1901-1961.

- *The Virginian* (1929)
- *A Farewell to Arms* (1932)
- *The Lives a Bengal Lancer* (1935)
- *The Plainsman* (1936)
- *The Westerner* (1940)
- *Unconquered* (1947)
- *Distant Drums* (1951)
- *Man of the West* (1958)
- *The Hanging Tree* (1959)

He won two best actor Academy Awards, first in 1942 for *Sergeant York* (1941) in which he portrayed Alvin York, the sympathetic contentious objector, who became America's most decorated military hero of World War I. He would win a second best acting Oscar in 1953 for his legendary performance as Marshal Will Kane in *High Noon* (1952). Cooper was nominated for three other best acting awards for:

- *Mr. Deeds Goes to Town* (1936)
- *The Pride of the Yankees* (1942)
- *For Whom the Bell Tolls* (1943)

In the Spring of 1960, he was diagnosed with prostate cancer and it was found to have spread to his colon. After a brief recovery in which he appeared to be healthy and strong, he returned to film *The Naked Edge* (1961). Shortly after completion of the film, he returned home and doctors found that the cancer had now spread to his lungs and bones. Cooper took his mortality in stride like the immortal Lou Gehrig, who he played in *Pride of the Yankees;* Cooper was quoted as saying, "If it's God will, that's all right too." Resigned to his fate, Cooper retired to his Holmby Hills, California, estate to wait for the inevitable.

At the Academy Awards ceremony on April 16, 1961, Cooper was honored with a lifetime achievement Oscar; an emotional and tear-filled Jimmy Stewart accepted the award on Cooper's behalf. He was unable to attend the event because of his failing health. Four weeks later, on May 13, 1961, with his family at his bedside, the legendary actor died. His funeral was held at the Church of the Good Shepherd in Beverly Hills, California. In attendance were over 400 mourners including numerous members of Hollywood's elite; among his pallbearers were good friends, Jack Benny and Jimmy Stewart.

To many people, Cooper's on-screen persona was erroneously perceived to be much like his real life and it was said that Gary Cooper as "himself" became one of Hollywood's most enduring symbols. But in reality, Cooper was an enigma, a study in contrasts, which unlike the wholesome characters he portrayed in his films, his real life was more complicated. It was alleged that throughout his film career he had numerous affairs with many of Hollywood's most famous leading actresses. Even with this tarnished personal image, Cooper remains one of Hollywood's legendary good guys and his films have lived on and become some of the classics of all-time.

Cooper was buried for thirteen years at Holy Cross Cemetery, Culver City, in the Grotto section, lot 194, space 5. He lay undisturbed until April 4, 1974, when his widow relocated his remains to Sacred Heart Cemetery, South Hampton, New York (Jesus and Mary section). Cooper's original burial plot at Holy Cross was vacant until 1976, and is now the final resting place of Mary Alice Hathaway.

Right:
Gary Cooper's former burial plot
at Holy Cross Catholic Cemetery;
against rocks, four markers from left:
Holy Cross Catholic Cemetery.

Joan Fontaine

(Born October 22, 1917 in Tokyo, Japan)

Best actress winner Joan Fontaine is still living and has been in retirement for many years, she last appeared on television in 1994, and her last motion picture was *The Witches* (1966). She is the younger sister of fellow actress and Academy Award winner, Olivia de Havilland.

Donald Crisp

(July 27, 1882 – May 25, 1974)

The accomplished director and character actor was born George William Crisp on July 27, 1882, in Abnerfeldy, Scotland (some sources show his birth place as London, England). He began his career in show business on stage but quickly moved to motion pictures as a director and as an actor. His earliest foray into film as an actor came in *The French Maid* (1908) and his directorial debut was *Her Father's Silent Partner* (1914). He played primarily father type characters and his slight brogue speech pattern added to a tender quality that made for some very memorable film roles. In his award winning film career, he directed over seventy films (primarily during the silent era, 1914-1930) and as an actor appeared in over 170 (1908-1963). Crisp's most famous film credits include:

- *Birth of a Nation* (1915)
- *The Return of Sherlock Holmes* (1929)
- *Mutiny on the Bounty* (1935)
- *Charge of the Light Brigade* (1936)
- *The Life of Emile Zola* (1937)
- *The Dawn Patrol* (1938)
- *Jezebel* (1938)
- *Wuthering Heights* (1939)
- *The Private Lives of Elizabeth and Essex* (1939)
- *Knute Rockne, All-American* (1940)
- *Lassie Come Home* (1943)
- *National Velvet* (1944)
- *Prince Valiant* (1954)

He won his first and only Academy Award for best supporting actor in 1942 for *How Green Was My Valley* (1941). After his wife, Jane Murfin's death in 1957, Crisp went into semi-retirement but returned to the screen shortly stating, "Idleness can ruin men." His last on-screen performance was in *Spencer's Mountain* (1963), co-starring Henry Fonda and Maureen O'Hara.

On May 25, 1974, Donald Crisp died from a stroke at the Van Nuys Community Hospital in Van Nuys, California. The actor had suffered several minor strokes in the previous year and was in failing health at the time of his death. His funeral service was held at the Church of the Recessional at Forest Lawn, Glendale.

Donald Crisp is buried in the Wee Kirk Church Yard, lot 2138, space 4 at Forest Lawn, Glendale.

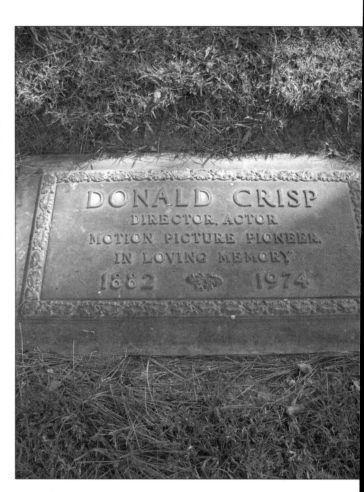

Donald Crisp's grave at Forest Lawn—Glendale.

Mary Astor

(May 3, 1903 – September 25, 1987)

"Five stages in the life of an actor: 1. Who's Mary Astor, 2. Get me Mary Astor, 3. Get me a Mary Astor type, 4. Get me a young Mary Astor, 5. Who's Mary Astor."

~Mary Astor

The talented but troubled award-winning actress of stage, screen, and television was born Lucile Vasconcellos Langhanke on May 3, 1906, in Quincy,

Illinois. Her path to Hollywood began at an early age with her parent's eager promotion. The young actress and her family moved to New York City in the early 1920s, where she was discovered by a Paramount Pictures talent scout. Her first screen appearance in 1920's *The Scarecrow* was only a bit part, but was just the beginning of a film career that spanned forty-four years (1920-1964), in which she would go on to star in nearly 150 films. In the early part of her career, she played innocent heroines in such films as *Beau Brummell* (1924), *Don Q Son of Zorro* (1925), and *Don Juan* (1926), but when talking pictures arrived, she began to play more sinister and evil characters in films such as *The Maltese Falcon* (1941) and *The Great Lie* (1941). In her later screen career, she played primarily mother roles in films such as *Thousand Cheers* (1943), *Meet Me in St. Louis* (1944), *Cynthia* (1947), and *Little Women* (1949). Other notable motion picture film credits include:

- *Man of Iron* (1935)
- *Brigham Young* (1940)
- *The Prisoner of Zenda* (1937)
- *Hush, Hush, Sweet Charlotte* (1964)

She won her first and only best supporting actress Academy Award in 1942, for *The Great Lie* (1941). After her award-winning performance, her film career began to fade, due to several failed marriages, scandal, bouts with alcoholism, depression, and attempted suicides. In 1935, during a bitter custody battle, following a divorce from her second husband, Frank Thorpe, a secret diary was admitted into evidence in which Mary, allegedly described in great detail (and in score card fashion), numerous sexual liaisons that occurred throughout the middle 1930s with many well-known leading men of the era. The diary was never made public and was destroyed after the court proceedings; Mary denied all of the charges and was eventually granted joint custody of her children. The damage had been done, her reputation had been tarnished, and her career was never the same.

Throughout the 1950s and 1960s, she appeared in numerous television programs and made her final on-screen performance as a cameo in 1964's thriller, *Hush, Hush, Sweet Charlotte*, after which she permanently retired from motion pictures. On September 25, 1987, while in residence at the Motion Picture and Television Country Home in Woodland Hills, California, she suffered a fatal heart attack.

Mary Astor is buried at Holy Cross Cemetery in Culver City, California, in lawn section N, lot 523, space 5.

Mary Astor, 1903-1987.

Mary Astor's final resting place at Holy Cross Catholic Cemetery.

John Ford

Best director John Ford's life and career achievements have been discussed in Chapter Two.

The Fifteenth Academy Awards Ceremony
"Garson's Filibuster"

A very patriotic crowd of stars, studio executives, and invited guests packed the Cocoanut Grove Ballroom at the Ambassador Hotel on the night of March 4, 1943, to honor films achievement for 1942. The host for a second year in a row was the incomparable, Bob Hope. His light-hearted wit and easy banter kept the evening flowing. There were plenty of political speeches, only to be interrupted by the occasional award presentation. There were no real surprises, with top film awards, but the evening will always be remembered for Greer Garson's long-winded acceptance speech for the best actress Oscar. Although, in reality, her speech lasted just shy of six minutes, those in attendance swore it had lasted for several hours. Her thoughts were heartfelt but it would go down in Academy lore as the longest acceptance speech. This speech would long haunt and forever symbolize Garson's very successful film career. The best film of 1942 went to William Wyler's, *Mrs. Miniver* (1942), a sentimental propaganda-like film, whose aim was to bring about the end of America's isolation during World War II. It garnered six Oscars, including best film, actress, supporting actress, and director.

The Nominees and Winners

Best Actor
Ronald Colman, **James Cagney**, Gary Cooper, Walter Pigeon, and Monty Woolley

Best Actress
Bette Davis, **Greer Garson**, Katharine Hepburn, Rosalind Russell, and Teresa Wright

Best Supporting Actor
William Bendix, **Van Heflin**, Walter Huston, Frank Morgan, and Henry Travers

Best Supporting Actress
Gladys Cooper, Agnes Moorehead, **Teresa Wright**, Susan Peters, and Dame May Whitty

Best Director
Michael Curtiz, John Farrow, Mervyn LeRoy, Sam Wood and **William Wyler**

James Cagney
(July 17, 1899 – March 30, 1986)

[About his most famous misquoted line:] *"I never actually said, 'Nnng-you dirty ra-at!' What I actually said was [imitating Cary Grant]: 'Judy! Judy! Judy!'"*
~James Cagney

The legendary tough guy of the silver screen was born on July 17, 1899, in New York City. The actor grew up in a tough area of the lower east side and Yorkville areas of Manhattan. It was here that he found the inspiration behind many of his unforgettable characters. While attending Columbia University, out of money and in need of a way to pay tuition, Cagney found a job as a dancer in a local vaudeville company. He was a good dancer and his talent did not go unnoticed. He would spend eleven years touring with small theater troops and vaudeville companies. Eventually, his hard work landed him a role on Broadway, where he was discovered.

The 15th Academy Awards, March 4, 1943; From left to right: Van Heflin, Greer Garson, James Cagney, and Teresa Wright. *Courtesy of the Herald Examiner Collection/ Los Angeles Public Library*

Al Jolson, the legendary actor of *The Jazz Singer* (1927), gave Cagney his big break in film, recommending to executives at Warner Studios, that he should play the role of Harry Delano in *Sinner's Holiday* (1930), a remake of the successful Broadway play, *Penny Arcade*. With this film's success, Cagney's Hollywood career was off and running. In five decades on the silver screen (1930-1984), Cagney would appear in over sixty motion pictures. But it wasn't until his fifth movie, *The Public Enemy* (1931) that he became a legend playing the unique role of the hard-hitting gangster, Tom Powers. The tough guy and rebellious characters that Cagney portrayed in his films throughout the 1930s were heartily embraced by Depression-era movie goers, whose personal lives had been ripped apart by uncertainty and economic chaos.

Some of Cagney's most memorable film credits include:

- *Blonde Crazy* (1931)
- *Hard to Handle* (1933)
- *Lady Killer* (1933)
- *G Men* (1935)
- *The Roaring Twenties* (1939)
- *Kiss Tomorrow Goodbye* (1950)
- *Mister Roberts* (1955)
- *The Gallant Hours* (1960)
- *Ragtime* (1981)

Did You Know?
Cagney turned down the role of Alfred P. Doolittle in *My Fair Lady* (1964), was a black belt in Judo, and was voted the 14th Greatest Movie Star of all-time by *Entertainment Weekly*.

Cagney won his only best actor Academy Award in 1943, returning to his song and dance roots, portraying legendary composer, James M. Cohan in *Yankee Doodle Dandy* (1942). He was the first actor to win the award for a musical role. Four years earlier, in 1939, Cagney had been nominated for his first best acting Oscar in *Angels with Dirty Faces* (1938) and honored again in 1956, for *Love Me or Leave Me* (1955).

By the early 1960s, Cagney had grown tired of film making and the studios. He felt that he had accomplished everything he wanted to in Hollywood and decided to retire. In 1981, after years away from Hollywood, and encouraged by his wife, Cagney accepted an offer from director Milos Forman to star in one last film, *Ragtime*. The film was critically well received and Cagney's performance was praised, but the rigors of travel and film schedules had once again forced the great actor into retirement, this time for good.

Five years later, on Easter Sunday, March 30, 1986, while staying at his beloved Duchess County farm house near Stanfordville, New York, the legendary actor died from a heart attack. He had been ill for many years, suffering from the effects of stroke, diabetes, and heart disease, and had only been released from a New York City hospital days before his death. His funeral was held at St. Francis de Sales Catholic Church in Manhattan, the same place where many years earlier, a young Cagney had been confirmed and served as an altar boy. The service was conducted by Cardinal John J. O'Conner and among the honored guests were New York Governor Mario Cuomo and New York Mayor Edward Koch. Pallbearers included dancer Mikhail Baryshnikov, boxer Floyd Patterson, and actor Ralph Bellamy.

James Cagney is interred at the Gate of Heaven Cemetery, Hawthorne, New York, in the St. Francis of Assisi mausoleum, M1, wing 5, corridor B, crypt 7C.

James Cagney's crypt at Gate of Heaven Cemetery.

Greer Garson

(September 29, 1904 – April 6, 1996)

[Speaking in the 1970s] *"I've been offered (roles as) nymphomaniacs, kleptomaniacs, pyromaniacs, homicidal maniacs and just plain maniacs. I think producers felt that after playing a long series of noble and admirable characters there would be quite a lot of shock value in seeing me play something altogether different. But I prefer upbeat stories that send people out of the theater feeling better than they did coming in. It's my cup of tea."*

~Greer Garson

The elegant and dignified redheaded actress was born Eileen Evelyn Greer Garson on September 29, 1904, in London, England. She never intended to become an actress, educated at London University. She aspired to be a school teacher, but ended up working in an advertising agency. To make ends meet, she sought out work as a part-time actress in small, local London theaters. She quickly gained a reputation as a talented actress and was discovered by MGM studio boss, Louis B. Mayer, while on a talent expedition in London. Signed to a contract by MGM, the vivacious actress took Hollywood by storm appearing for the first time on screen in 1939's *Goodbye, Mr. Chip's*, in which she garnered the first of seven best actress Oscar nominations. In a television and film career that spanned four decades (1939-1982), she appeared in only twenty-four feature motion pictures. She often played a courageous mother character, but in later years was able to break out of this type casting to play comedic and other forms of dramatic parts. She was often paired with actor Walter Pigeon, and the two appeared together in eight motion pictures.

She won the golden statuette only once in 1943 for her portrayal of the courageous house wife, Mrs. Miniver in *Mrs. Miniver* (1942). Her other Academy Award nominated films are:

- *Blossoms in the Dust* (1941)
- *Madame Curie* (1943)
- *Mrs. Parkington* (1944)
- *Valley of Decision* (1945)
- *Sunrise at Campobello* (1960)

By the late 1940s, her film career began to wane with less than spectacular box office successes. In 1960, she made a comeback with *Sunrise at Campbello* (considered by many to be her best performance) but this new-found success was short lived and she soon found herself with few opportunities. She retired in the late 1960s with her husband Buddy Fogelson to their New Mexico ranch.

Did You Know?
Garson was offered and turned down the role of Joan Collins mother in television's *Dynasty* (1981) and that she along with actress Bette Davis share the record for most consecutive Oscar nominations (five).

In the 1980s, she suffered from chronic heart problems which drastically slowed her environmental and charity work. She underwent quadruple bypass heart surgery in 1988. On April 6, 1996, while in residence at the Dallas Presbyterian Hospital, she had another heart attack and died.

Greer Garson's final resting place is found in the Fogelson family plot at Sparkman Hill Crest Memorial Park in Dallas, Texas.

Greer Garson, 1904-1996.

Van Heflin

(December 13, 1910 – July 23, 1971)

The talented character actor who often played tough guys with a sensitive and often vulnerable side was born Emmett Evan Heflin, Jr. on December 13, 1910, in Walters, Oklahoma. In his youth, Heflin worked as a merchant marine and got his start in show business by accident while on shore leave in New York City. He was discovered by Broadway director Richard Boleslawski, who cast him in the play, *Mr. Moneypenny*. The play closed after a short run, and he returned to the sea but the acting bug had been planted. Three years later, Heflin returned state side, and enrolled in drama school. In 1936, after a successful run in which he appeared in eight Broadway plays, Heflin made the switch to motion pictures, and was quickly signed by RKO Pictures, and appeared in his first film, *A Woman Rebels* (1936). In a memorable screen career that included over fifty motion pictures from 1936 to 1971, Heflin's most unforgettable movie credits include:

- *The Outcasts of Poker Flat* (1937)
- *Santa Fe Trail* (1940)
- *The Three Musketeers* (1948)
- *Shane* (1953)
- *Battle Cry* (1955)
- *The Greatest Story Ever Told* (1965)
- *Airport* (1970)

Van Helfin, 1910-1971.

Heflin won the best supporting actor Academy Award in 1943, for his portrayal of the hard drinking stooge, Jeff Harnett in *Johnny Eager* (1942). He almost always played the supporting role in films, his rugged characters seemed to possess a certain vulnerability that showed weakness which often lead his characters into dire circumstances.

Did You Know?

MGM studio head, Louis B. Mayer, (upon meeting Heflin for the first time and commenting about his on-screen characters), took one look at Heflin and said, "You will never get the girl in the end," to which Heflin sarcastically replied, "So, I guess I have to work on my acting."

Heflin was an ardent health fanatic in his later years and often swam laps in his Los Angeles area apartment pool. On June 6, 1971, while completing his regular swimming routine, he suffered a heart attack. He was able to get to the side of the pool and hang onto a ladder but was unsuccessful in getting out of the water. Fellow tenants helped pull the stricken actor from the water but when paramedics finally arrived, he was unconsciousness and unresponsive. Heflin was transported to Citizens Emergency Hospital in Hollywood, where he lay in a coma for forty-seven days. The award-winning actor died on July 23, 1971, at age sixty, never having regained consciousness.

Van Heflin's remains were cremated and scattered in the Pacific Ocean.

Teresa Wright

(October 27, 1918 – March 6, 2005)

"I only ever wanted to be an actress, not a star."
~Teresa Wright

The award-winning actress who often played the sweet, pretty girl-next-door role was born Muriel Teresa Wright on October 27, 1918, in the borough of Harlem, New York. Her parents divorced when she was very young, and she moved often, living with various relatives. Wright began acting at an early age and she had great success on the Broadway stage. She was discovered by MGM talent scouts and offered a contract by Samuel Goldwyn. Her first film in 1941,

The Little Foxes, garnered a best supporting actress Oscar nomination in her sophomore effort, for *Mrs. Miniver* (1942), she won the best supporting actress Academy Award, and in her third effort, *The Pride of the Yankees* (1942) she was nominated for a best lead actress Oscar. She is the only actress in Academy Award history to be nominated three times for her first three films.

Her fourth movie, Alfred Hitchcock's, *Shadow of a Doubt* (1943), did not earn an award nomination but was a classic. This was followed up by *Casanova Brown* (1944) and *The Best Years of Our Lives* (1946). Wright's career had an unprecedented meteoric rise but she did not want any part of the typical Hollywood publicity and often refused to participate in photo shoots or magazine interviews. She would only accept roles as the wholesome daughter, wife, or sweetheart, but never the seductress.

Did You Know?
When Wright died in 2005, and in honor of her performance as Lou Gehrig's wife in *The Pride of the Yankees* (1942), her name was announced at Yankee Stadium during the roll call of Yankee ballplayers who had passed away in the previous year.

At first, MGM was understanding and tolerant of Ms. Wright's attitude, but this wore thin and eventually totally eroded. The situation culminated in 1948, when MGM head Samuel Goldwyn's patience ran out and he fired the talented but difficult actress for "uncooperative" behavior. Her career would survive, but motion pictures were not as forthcoming and she turned to television and the stage. Wright's successful television and motion picture career spanned five decades, from 1941 to 1997, which included over eighty roles. Her last film appearance was in John Grisham's *Rainmaker* (1997), after which she permanently retired. The Academy Award winning actress died on March 6, 2005, at the Yale-New Haven Hospital in New Haven, Connecticut, from a heart attack.

Wright's body was donated to the Yale University Medical School for research and final disposition of her remains are unknown.

Teresa Wright,
1918-2005.

William Wyler

(July 1, 1902 – July 27, 1981)

One of the greatest motion picture film directors of all-time was born Willi Wyler on July 1, 1902, in Mulhouse, Alsace, Germany (now Haut-Rhin, France). He immigrated to the United States in 1920 at the age of eighteen to work for his cousin, Universal Studios boss Carl Laemmle. He quickly rose through the ranks at the studio, and by 1925, was given the opportunity to direct a film, *Crook Buster* (1925). In 1930, he made his first commercially successful "A" level film, *Hell's Heroes* (1930). This film was Universal's first all-sound movie and was shot entirely on location. Wyler established himself as an "A" list director in the 1930s and became one of producer Samuel Goldwyn's favorite directors. In an award-winning film career that spanned forty-five years (1925-1970), Wyler amassed an impressive film repertoire of over seventy motion picture credits that include *Her First Mate* (1933), *Jezebel* (1938), *The Memphis Belle* (1944), *Big Country* (1958), and *Funny Girl* (1968).

Wyler was nominated for twelve best directing Oscars, winning the gold statuette three times. His Academy Award nominated films include:

- *Dodsworth* (1936)
- *Wuthering Heights* (1939)
- *The Letter* (1940)
- *The Little Foxes* (1941)
- *The Heiress* (1949)
- *Detective Story* (1951
- *Roman Holiday* (1953)
- *Friendly Persuasion* (1956)
- *The Collector* (1965)

His Academy Award winning films were:

- *Mrs. Miniver* (1942)
- *The Best Years of Our Lives* (1946)
- *Ben-Hur* (1959)

Did You Know?

Wyler was originally set to direct *The Sound of Music* (1965) but pulled out because he found what he thought was a more worthy project *The Collector* (1965). Bette Davis credits him with making her a box office star in the film, *Jezebel* (1938), for which she won an Oscar.

Known to be hard on actors, Wyler often made them repeat scenes with little or no input, earning the nick-name "90-take Wyler." He believed that after getting the actor angry, they would shed their preconceived ideas of what a scene should be and play it at a truer level. These techniques often caused his films to go over budget and schedule but it produced great films. Wyler demanded a lot from his actors and even more from his audiences, who he likened to being intelligent collaborators.

Wyler directed his last film, *The Liberation of L.B. Jones* (1970), and due to failing health, retired from film making. He died on July 27, 1981, at his Beverly Hills, California, home of a massive heart attack at the age of seventy-nine. A memorial service was held at the Directors Guild Theater in Hollywood on August 1, 1981. In attendance were over 400 mourners which included many members of the Hollywood elite.

William Wyler is interred at Forest Lawn Memorial Park, Glendale in the Eventide lawn, lot 2998, space 2.

Director William Wyler's final resting place at Forest Lawn—Glendale.

The Sixteenth Academy Awards Ceremony
"A New Beginning"

For the first time, the awards ceremony was open to the public, Bette Davis had won her battle, and hundreds of tickets were handed out to service men and women. It was also the first time the event would be an actual show and not a dinner banquet. Hollywood wanted to show how it could entertain the troops, and the ceremony would be forever changed. In deference to the ongoing war effort, there were no jeweled gowns, tuxedos, or even cocktails served at the event. It was held on March 2, 1944, at Grauman's Chinese Theater in Hollywood and the host for the night was comedian Jack Benny. The best picture went to the box office smash, *Casablanca* (1943), starring Humphrey Bogart. This film was initially seen as a dark horse to win the honor, because there were other far more sentimental and patriotic war films and Hollywood saw itself as the fourth wing of the armed forces. In the end, *Casablanca* won. It is ironic that this film did not garner any of the best acting awards even though it did win best film.

The Nominees and Winner

Best Actor
Humphrey Bogart, Gary Cooper, **Paul Lukas**, Walter Pigeon, and Mickey Rooney

Best Actress
Jean Arthur, Ingrid Bergman, Joan Fontaine, Greer Garson, and **Jennifer Jones**

Best Supporting Actor
Charles Bickford, **Charles Colburn**, J. Carrol Naish, Claude Rains, and Akim Tamiroff

Best Supporting Actress
Gladys Cooper, Paulette Goddard, **Katina Paxinou**, Anne Revere, and Lucille Watson

Best Director
Clarence Brown, **Michael Curtiz**, Henry King, Ernest Lubitsch, and George Stevens

Paul Lukas
(May 26, 1891 – August 16, 1971)

The suave and debonair award-winning actor was born Pal Lukacs on May 26, 1891, in Budapest, Hungry. In 1911, at the age twenty, he joined the national theater of Budapest and after a successful run in the theater, arrived in Hollywood in 1927. His Hungarian accent was no problem with silent films but when the talkies arrived, he had to learn English, which he did without any problems. In a prolific show business career that spanned forty-two years, 1928 to 1970, Lukas appeared in over 100 motion pictures and television programs, and during this film career, he played primarily continental playboys or sophisticated villains. His major film credits include:

- *Two Lovers* (1928)
- *Unfaithful* (1931)
- *Little Women* (1933)
- *The Countess Monte Cristo* (1934)
- *The Three Musketeers* (1935)
- *The Lady Vanishes* (1938)
- *20,000 Leagues Under the Sea* (1954)
- *Tender is the Night* (1962)

In 1941, Lukas won the New York Drama League Award for his Broadway stage role as the virtuous ant-Nazi spy, Kurt Muller on *Watch on the Rhine;* the following year in 1943, he reprised this role on film and won a best lead actor Oscar. It was noted by numerous people that the actor was so mystified when he won the award that he almost dropped the statuette.

In April of 1971, the talented actor retired from film and moved to Tangier, Morocco, and after only four months on August 16, 1971, suffered a fatal heart attack at a local Tangier hospital.

Paul Lukas' funeral arrangements and burial location are unknown.

Jennifer Jones
(March 2, 1919 – December 17, 2009)

A passionate, yet sensitive actress, Jennifer Jones was born Phylis Lee Isley on March 2, 1919, in Tulsa, Oklahoma. She became interested in acting at an early age, eventually studying acting at both Northwestern University and the American Academy of Dramatic Arts in New York. After several failed attempts to break into film, she settled in New York. Her big break came in 1943, when she met her future husband, producer David O. Selznick, who cast her in *The Song of Bernadette* (1943). Selznick began to groom his new protégé for stardom, carefully choosing her roles and eventually marrying the actress in 1949. Their union would last fifteen years until his death in 1965.

One of Hollywood's most underrated award-winning actresses, Jones' film career would span twenty-plus years (1943-1974); she appeared in twenty seven films that include:

- *Madame Bovary* (1949)
- *The Wild Heart* (1952)
- *Ruby Gentry* (1952)
- *A Farewell to Arms* (1957)
- *Tender is the Night* (1962)
- *The Towering Inferno* (1974)

She was nominated for five Academy Awards, winning for best actress in 1944 (in her debut film), *The Song of Bernadette* (1943). She was nominated again in 1945 in a supporting role for *Since You Went Away* (1944), and for a third consecutive year (1946) was nominated for a best lead actress Oscar for *Love Letters* (1945). In 1947 and 1956, she was again nominated for best actress Oscars for *Duel in the Sun* (1946) and *Love is a Many Splendored Thing* (1955).

Despite her successes in Hollywood, Jones remained a very private person. This caused her to be less noticed and her film career began to wane. In 1974, after filming *The Towering Inferno*, Jones decided to permanently retire from film making and instead concentrate on philanthropic work. She had married industrialist and art collector, Norton Simon in 1971 and the pair started the Norton Simon Foundation and Art Museum in Pasadena, California. No stranger to mental health issues, Jones attempted suicide in 1967 by taking an overdose of drugs and in 1976, her daughter, Mary J. Selznick, committed suicide, after which, Jones became an advocate for mental health issues. Jennifer Jones died on December 17, 2009, from natural causes at her home in Malibu, California.

Jennifer Jones' cremated remains were given to family and final disposition is unknown. It has been speculated that she may be interred with her second husband, David O. Selznick, and their daughter in the Great Mausoleum at Forest Lawn, Glendale. This is only conjecture because the public is no longer allowed access to the building and the cemetery will not divulge any information. Her third husband, Norton Simon's ashes were scattered at sea.

Did You Know?
The Oscar statuettes this year were made out of plaster because metal was scarce, and that for the first time, best supporting actors and actresses received full size awards, rather than miniature plaques.

Jennifer Jones, 1919-2009.

Charles Coburn

(June 19, 1877 – August 30, 1961)

"Don't ever believe that beauty and charm are the exclusive property of youth. Like smooth brandy, sex appeal improves with age."

~Charles Coburn

The venerable character actor who was known for his monocle, aristocratic southern style, and sly sense of humor was born June 19, 1877, in Savannah, Georgia. He began a very successful acting career in the theater at age fourteen. The bright lights of Hollywood did not beckon until 1938; the actor, then nearly sixty, was a veteran of the Broadway stage but was a new comer to film. From 1937 to 1961, Coburn made over ninety motion pictures and television appearances. In 1944, he won the best supporting actor Academy Award for *The More the Merrier* (1943), playing the charming and funny, Benjamin Dingle. In his acceptance speech (making fun of his own advanced age) said that he hoped that in another fifty years time, the children and children's children of the present Academy voters would again honor him and his acting skill with another Oscar statuette.

In a career in motion pictures that only spanned two decades, Coburn's most memorable film credits include:

- *Of Human Hearts* (1938)
- *Vivacious Lady* (1938)
- *The Lady Eve* (1941)
- *The Devil and Mrs. Jones* (1941)
- *Kings Row* (1942)
- *Heaven Can Wait* (1943)
- *Rhapsody in Blue* (1945)
- *The Green Years* (1946)
- *Gentlemen Prefer Blondes* (1953)
- *Around the World in Eighty Days* (1956)

In his personal life, he had been a widower for twenty-two years, when in 1959, he met and married Winifred Natzka, a young woman half his age. The actor loved life and as his eightieth year approached, lived it to the fullest. A ball of energy, he would bounce around all day, enjoying lunch with friends, dancing, and stayed up late with old cronies playing poker. On August 30, 1961, while between stage plays, Coburn underwent minor throat surgery at Lennox Hill Hospital in New York City; during this procedure he suffered a fatal heart attack.

After his death, controversy erupted as to what to do with the actors cremated remains. In his will he expressly wished not to have a funeral or memorial service and wanted his ashes scattered at several different locations, that included the foot of the Edwin Booth statue in Gramercy Park, the memorial tree to his first wife (also in Gramercy Park), his parent's grave in Savannah, and along the Mohawk Trail in Albany, New York. Under the laws of New York and Georgia, this was not legally permissible and it is unknown if the executors of Coburn's estate actually followed through with his final wishes.

Edwin Booth statute in Gramercy Park, where the ashes of Charles Colburn were allegedly scattered.

Katina Paxinou

(December 17, 1900 – February 22, 1973)

The fiery actress of both the Greek stage and American cinema was born Ekaterini Konstantopoulou on December 17, 1900, in Piraeus, Greece. She first appeared on the Greek stage in 1927 and by the 1930s was one of the founding members of the Greek Royal Theater. When World War II broke out, Paxinou immigrated to Great Britain, and then to the United States. She first appeared on screen in 1943's *For Whom the Bells Toll*, in which she played the Spanish Civil War revolutionary, Pilar. It was for this role, that Paxinou won the best supporting actress Oscar for 1944.

Did You Know?

Paxinou was a political radical, who was a member of the Greek underground movement that opposed the Nazi regime during World War II and was the first non-American actress to win a best supporting actress Oscar.

In a very short film career, Paxinou only appeared in fourteen motion pictures from 1943 to 1970, returning to the stage and her native Greece in the early 1950s. Her most notable film credits include:

- *Confidential Agent* (1943)
- *Hostages* (1943)
- *Prince of Foxes* (1949)
- *Mourning Becomes Electra* (1947)
- *The Miracle* (1959)

On February 22, 1973, while at a local Athens hospital, Paxinou died from cancer at age seventy-three.

Katina Paxinou's grave is found in Athens, Greece at the First Cemetery of Athens.

Michael Curtiz

(December 24, 1886 – April 10, 1962)

One of the most prolific and successful directors of the golden age of cinema, Curtiz was born Mano Kertesz Kaminer on December 24, 1886, in Budapest, Hungry. Information about his early career is sparse. What is known is that he began as an actor and director at the National Hungarian Theater in 1912. During the early 1920s, he directed numerous successful films, both in Denmark and Hungry. His film *Moon of Israel* (1924) caught the eye of Jack Warner of Warner Studios, he moved to the United States, changed his name to Michael Curtiz, and in 1926, made his first American film, *The Third Degree*.

He was a tough director, and often offended those he was working with. Curtiz demanded perfection from actors in his films and often had a low opinion of them in general. His films spanned all types and genres and he thrived at Warner Studios during the 1930s and 1940s. In a film career that spanned thirty-five years (1926-1961), Curtiz directed over 100 feature motion pictures that included some of the greatest films of all time:

- *Noah's Ark* (1928)
- *River's End* (1930)
- *The Woman from Monte Carlo* (1932)
- *Mystery of the Wax Museum* (1933)
- *Charge of the Light Brigade* (1936)
- *Anthony Adverse* (1936)
- *The Adventures of Robin Hood* (1938)
- *Dodge City* (1939)
- *The Private Lives of Elizabeth and Essex* (1939)
- *The Sea Hawk* (1940)
- *Mildred Pierce* (1945)
- *Flamingo Road* (1949)
- *White Christmas* (1954)
- *We're No Angels* (1955)
- *King Creole* (1958)
- *The Hangman* (1959)
- *The Adventures of Huckleberry Finn* (1960)
- *The Comancheros* (1961)

He was nominated for four best directing Academy Awards:

- *Captain Blood* (1935)
- *Four Daughters* (1938)
- *Angels with Dirty Faces* (1938)
- *Yankee Doodle Dandy* (1942)

...and won the Oscar in 1943 for *Casablanca*, which is arguably one of the greatest films ever made.

Curtiz was married and divorced three times; he had at least two illegitimate children from relationships prior to arriving in the United States. His third wife Bess Meredyth was a successful actress, screen writer and one of the original thirty-six members of the Academy of Motion Picture Arts and Sciences. Their forty-year marriage was volatile and endured numerous bouts of infidelity and domestic abuse by Curtiz. But through all this pain and suffering Meredyth stayed with Curtiz, often serving as his assistant on film sets. It wasn't until shortly before his death from cancer in 1961, with Curtiz bedridden, that she got the nerve to leave.

The award-winning director died on April 10, 1962 from cancer.

Michael Curtiz is buried at Forest Lawn, Glendale, in the Whispering Pines lawn, lot 1178, space 5.

The grave of director Michael Curtiz at Forest Lawn—Glendale.

The Seventeenth Academy Awards Ceremony
"Everything Going Its Way"

The award ceremony was held on March 15, 1945, and for a second year in a row at Grauman's Chinese Theater. The co-masters of ceremony were Bob Hope and director John Cromwell. There were no surprises in the races as to who would win the coveted Oscar statuettes. Bing Crosby, the legendary crooner, was nominated for best actor but did not take the nomination seriously. In fact, Crosby did not plan on attending the ceremony and was on a local Los Angeles golf course the day of the event, when he was persuaded by his mother that he needed to be present at the ceremony. He arrived late, but was able to accept his best acting award. Crosby said upon accepting his award, "I couldn't be more surprised if I won the Kentucky Derby. Can you imagine the jokes Hope's going to write about this in his radio show?" Bob Hope then quipped, "Crosby winning an Oscar is like hearing Sam Goldwyn is lecturing at Oxford." The successful duo of Hope and Crosby would make numerous "road" films over a period of twenty years (1941-1961). The best film of 1944 was not a big surprise. The Oscar went to *Going My Way*, the warm hearted story of a young progressive Catholic priest (Bing Crosby), who matches ideas and wits with an older priest (Barry Fitzgerald).

Winner and Nominees

Best Actor
Charles Boyer, **Bing Crosby**, Barry Fitzgerald, Cary Grant, and Alexander Knox

Best Actress
Ingrid Bergman, Claudette Colbert, Bette Davis, Greer Garson, and Barbara Stanwyck

Best Supporting Actor
Hume Cronyn, **Barry Fitzgerald**, Claude Rains, Clifton Webb, and Monty Woolley

Best Supporting Actress
Ethel Barrymore, Angela Lansbury, Aline MacMahon, Jennifer Jones, and Agnes Moorehead

Best Director
Alfred Hitchcock, Henry King, **Leo McCarey**, Otto Preminger, and Billy Wilder

Bing Cosby

(May 2, 1903 – October 14, 1977)

"There's nothing in this world I wouldn't do for (Bob) Hope, and there is nothing he wouldn't do for me…we spend our lives doing nothing for each other."

~Bing Crosby

The singer, comedian, and actor was born Harry Lillis Crosby on May 2, 1903, in Tacoma, Washington. His trade mark nickname "Bing" was a derivative of a character named "Bingo" in the comic strip "Bingville Bugle;" the comic strip was a favorite of the young crooner. He never formally studied music but in his first year of college, with a few buddies, formed a small band called the "Musicaladers." The group had some success and it was decided that they would go to Los Angeles and pursue a vaudeville career. During a successful two-year tour of the country under the name "The Rhythm Boys," they were discovered by band leader Paul Whiteman. Bing and his band mates toured with Whiteman for three years and it was with this band that Bing got his first taste of Hollywood, appearing in Whiteman's motion picture, *King of Jazz* (1930). Bing and the Rhythm Boys then joined band leader Gus Arnheim at the Cocoanut Ballroom at the Ambassador Hotel in Los Angeles.

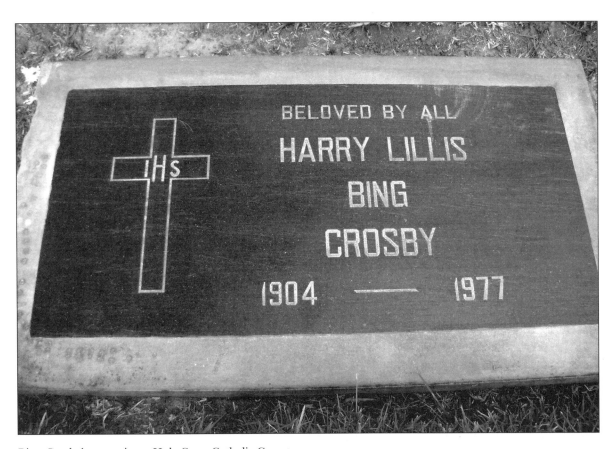

Bing Crosby's gravesite at Holy Cross Catholic Cemetery.

Bing Crosby, scrap rubber drive during World War II (June 15, 1942). *Courtesy of the Franklin D. Roosevelt Library and Museum (Public domain photographs, 1882-1962)*

It was here that Bing became known to the Hollywood crowd, and it was Mack Sennett, who signed him to a contract with Paramount Pictures. In a series of short subject films, Crosby was heard singing and this lead to his first musical recording contract with Brunswick Records. Later, a regular singing gig developed with CBS Radio and shows at the Paramount Theater in New York City. Moving back to the West Coast in 1932, Crosby appeared in his first feature film role, *The Big Broadcast*, a motion picture that would launch him into super stardom. Crosby would go on to appear in over fifty feature films, including twenty "Road" movies in which he appeared with his good friend, Bob Hope.

His most famous movie role was that of Father O'Malley in *Going My Way* (1944), for which he won the best actor Academy Award. He would go on to recreate the successful role in two subsequent films, *The Bells of St. Mary's* (1945), and *Say One for Me* (1959), his other notable motion picture film credits include:

- *Too Much Harmony* (1933)
- *Mississippi* (1935)
- *Anything Goes* (1936)
- *Pennies From Heaven* (1936)
- *Holiday Inn* (1942)
- *A Connecticut Yankee in King Arthur's Court* (1949)
- *The Country* Girl (1954)
- *High Society* (1956)

Another of Crosby's most famous movies is the holiday favorite, *White Christmas* (1954); in it he sings the title track from the film—Irving Berlin's "White Christmas." This song became his most popular and recognizable hit of his musical career. Crosby was nominated for two additional best actor Academy Awards for *The Bell's of St. Mary's* (1945) and *The Country Girl* (1954).

Did You Know?
Crosby and actress Grace Kelly (the future Princess of Monaco) had a love affair after co-starring in *The Country Girl* (1954) and this delayed his second marriage to actress Kathryn Grant until 1957. His trade mark large ears were often taped back for his screen roles.

Crosby's personal life was not as successful as his professional one; in 1943, his Toluca Lake home was destroyed by fire, in 1952, his first wife Dixie Lee, died at the age of forty from cancer, he was criticized by his eldest son, Gary, in his book *Going My Own Way* (1983), in which Bing was characterized as an abusive and violent father. His four sons from his first marriage all died tragically, Lindsay and Dennis committed suicide, Gary from lung cancer, and Phillip from a heart attack.

Did You Know?
Bob Hope dismissed Gary Crosby's tell-all book, saying, "Bing tortured me all the time with his singing, but I never wrote a book about it."

In 1957, Crosby married for a second time; Kathryn Grant was a young actress thirty years his junior. The couple had three children, Harry, Nathaniel, and Mary, the latter is an actress of some note. It is speculated that because of Crosby's regret over the way he treated his first family, he became a better husband and doting father the second time around.

On October 14, 1977, after finishing an eighteen-hole round of golf in Madrid, Spain, the acclaimed actor collapsed and died from a massive heart attack. He was in Spain for some rest and relaxation after completing a successful run at the London Palladium. He died while doing what he loved best. Golf was his passion. His body was flown back to the United States accompanied by his eldest son, Gary. A private funeral mass for only immediate family and few close friends, including Bob Hope, was held in the rectory chapel of St. Paul the Apostle Catholic Church in Westwood. The forty-minute service included organ music in which some of Bing's greatest hits were played.

Bing Crosby is buried at Holy Cross Cemetery, Culver City, in the grotto, lot 119, space one, next to his first wife, Dixie Lee.

Ingrid Bergman

(August 29, 1915 – August 29, 1982)

"I don't regret a thing I've done. I only regret the things I didn't do."

~Ingrid Bergman

The charming and sometimes unaffected actress, who enraptured audiences with her courage though scandal and turmoil, was born August 29, 1915, in Stockholm, Sweden. Bergman decided to become an actress after finishing her formal schooling. She did not have an affinity for the stage, but instead found her true calling in film acting. She was discovered by famed American film producer, David O. Selznick, who signed the Swedish actress to a contract with United Artists studios. Her first American film was a remake of a Swedish motion picture, *Intermezzo: A Love Story* (1939); in it she successfully reprised the role of Anita Hoffman, she had played while in Sweden. Bergman was about to take Hollywood by storm and from 1939 to 1982, appeared in over forty feature films. Her most memorable film credits include:

- *Dr. Jekyll and Mr. Hyde* (1941)
- *Spell Bound* (1945)
- *Notorious* (1946)
- *Stromboli* (1950)
- *Good Bye Again* (1961)
- *A Walk in the Spring Rain* (1970)

Her film career often mirrored her personal life; early film roles saw her cast as a sweet woman, who was dominated by men, then she took on characters that were of an independent nature, and finally, she evolved into a woman of insight and strength. She was the winner of the three best lead actress Oscars, first in 1945 for:

- *Gaslight* (1944)
- 1957 for *Anastasia* (1956)
- 1975 for *Murder on the Orient Express* (1974)

Her Academy Award best actress nominated films were:

- *For Whom the Bells Toll* (1943)
- *The Bells of St. Mary's* (1945)
- *Joan of Arc* (1948)
- *Hostsonaten* (1978)

These Academy Award winning motion pictures followed the growth of her practiced and personal development. The public could not get enough of the talented actress, enthralled and obsessed with her every move. Bergman will always be remembered as Humphrey Bogart's love interest, Lisa Lund, in the legendary, *Casablanca* (1942).

> ## Did You Know?
> Bergman's famous love affair with World War II photographer, Robert Capa, was the basis for Alfred Hitchcock's film *Rear Window* (1954) and is the mother of famed model/actress, Isabella Rossellini.

In 1948, the so called "scandal of the century" hit; Bergman was at the peak of her Hollywood popularity when she began a torrid love affair with director Roberto Rossellini while filming *Stromboli* in Italy. Bergman became pregnant with Rossellini's child and bore a son out of wedlock. The problem was that at the time of the affair Bergman was married to another man, Peter Lindstrom. This was a scandal of unbelievable proportions; the media had a field day, and Bergman's image of the wholesome, virtuous woman was all but destroyed. Her marriage to Lindstrom was shattered and ended in divorce. Soon after, she married Rossellini but the damage had already been done. Their union would produce two more children. Sadly in 1957, this marriage also ended in divorce.

Bergman's career was damaged by the scandal but she survived and went on to have other great successes in film, television, and stage. The last role before her death, Bergman played famed Israeli Prime Minster, Golda Meir in the 1982, television mini-series, *A Woman Called Golda* and for which she was posthumously awarded a best actress, Emmy Award. On August 29, 1982, (her sixty-seventh birthday) Bergman died after a long battle with breast cancer at her London apartment. She had battled the disease for eight years, having undergone mastectomies in 1974 and 1978. At her bedside when she passed was her third husband, Lars Schmidt. Even though the pair had divorced in 1975, they remained close friends. No public funeral was held for Bergman, a small service for family was held at a London area crematory.

Ingrid Bergman, 1915-1982.

Left to right: Samuel Goldwyn, Ingrid Bergman (seated), unknown producer (behind) and Roberto Rossellini. Circa, 1949. *Courtesy of the Security Pacific National Bank Collection/ Los Angeles Public Library*

Per her final wishes, Bergman's body was cremated, some of her ashes were scattered at sea off the coast of Sweden and the remainder were buried next to her parents at the Northern Cemetery (Norra Begravingsplatsen) in Solna, Sweden. The unassuming grave is found in section Kv 11F, space 228/11573 and her epitaph simply reads, (in script) Ingrid, 1915-1982.

Barry Fitzgerald

(March 10, 1888 – January 14, 1961)

One of the all-time great character actors in Hollywood history was born William Joseph Shields on March 10, 1888, in Dublin, Ireland. The diminutive Irishman with the irresistible brogue did not start acting until late in life (age forty). Fitzgerald quit his job as a civil servant in Dublin to perform on the London stage with the Abbey Players. In 1930, he made his Hollywood film debut in Alfred Hitchcock's, *Juno and the Paycock* but did not appear in another film for six years, when in 1936, he was coaxed by director John Ford into appearing in *The Plough and the Stars*. After, his big screen career took off and from 1930 to 1959, Fitzgerald appeared in over forty motion pictures, some of which include:

- *Bringing Up Baby* (1938)
- *The Dawn Patrol* (1938)
- *How Green Was My Valley* (1941)
- *Two Years Before the Mast* (1946)
- *The Naked City* (1948)
- *Union Station* (1950)
- *The Quiet Man* (1952)

In his many film roles, Fitzgerald usually played the archetypical Irishman or the affable clergyman and with his scene stealing grin that was an audience favorite.

Tragedy struck on March 17, 1944, when the veteran actor hit two pedestrians, (killing one and severely injuring another) while driving his car on Hollywood Boulevard, near Sycamore Street. There was no evidence of drug or alcohol use and it appeared to be just a tragic accident, but an overzealous Los Angeles District Attorney's office still filed a complaint, charging Fitzgerald with vehicular manslaughter. The actor was arrested, booked, and a trial date was set for January 9, 1945. At this hearing, Superior Court Judge William McKay dismissed the charges against Fitzgerald for lack of evidence.

> **Did You Know?**
> Fitzgerald's brother is noted actor Arthur Shields and the two siblings appeared in several films together most notably, *The Quiet Man* (1952). Arthur Shields died in 1970, and is buried next to his brother.

Two short months later on March 15, 1945, at the annual Academy Awards ceremony, Fitzgerald was on top of the world when he became the first actor to be nominated for a best lead and supporting actor award for the same movie, *Going My Way* (1944). He lost the lead actor Oscar to his co-star Bing Crosby but took home the best supporting actor statuette. The following year, the Academy board of directors changed the rules, not allowing an actor or actress to be nominated for the same role in two different acting categories in the same movie.

In October of 1959, Fitzgerald underwent a brain operation for an undisclosed illness; this left him incapacitated and unable to care for himself. The last two years of his life were spent in a Dublin area nursing home and he died on January 14, 1961, at Dublin's St. Patrick's Hospital from a heart attack at age seventy-two. His funeral was held in Dublin at St. Patrick's Protestant Church of Ireland; in attendance were numerous personalities of the stage and government.

He is buried at Deansgrange Cemetery in Dublin, Ireland, and his tombstone epitaph is inscribed with his given name of William J. Shields.

Ethel Barrymore

(August 15, 1879 – June 18, 1959)

"To be a success, an actress must have the face of Venus, the brain of Minerva, the grace of Terpsichore, the memory of Macaulay, the figure of Juno and the hide of a rhinoceros."

~Ethel Barrymore

Ethel Barrymore was the second child of three siblings who would form one of Hollywood's greatest acting families. She was born on August 15, 1879, in Philadelphia, Pennsylvania, and was destined to become an actress. Her entire family, including both parents and her two brothers, Lionel and John, all became famous actors. Ethel made her stage debut in 1894, in New York City and was an immediate sensation. She had a warm and affectionate persona and her onstage charisma enchanted American theater fans. Even though the theater was her first love, she moved into films and, even though she did not achieve the level of super stardom of her brothers, she was able to win over movie-going audiences. Ethel Barrymore's famed motion picture career spanned four decades from 1914 to 1957, in which she appeared in thirty-seven films some of which include:

- *The Nightingale* (1914)
- *The Divorcee* (1919)
- *Camille* (1926)
- *The Farmers Daughter* (1947)
- *Moonrise* (1948)
- *The Midnight Kiss* (1949)
- *Just for You* (1952)
- *Young at Heart* (1954)

Did You Know?

Ethel Barrymore once turned down a proposal from a young Winston Churchill (she thought he had no real future). She only appeared in one film with her two famous brothers, *Rasputin and the Empress* (1932). She is also the great-aunt of actress Drew Barrymore.

Known as the consummate actress, she worked steadily in film throughout the 1940s and 1950s, often playing the role of the witty elderly mother, grandmother, or grand dame. She won the best supporting actress Oscar in 1945 for her portrayal of Ma Mott in *None but the Lonely Heart* (1944). She would go on to be nominated for three more best supporting actress Academy Awards:

- *The Spiral Staircase* (1945)
- *The Paradine Case* (1947)
- *Pinky* (1949)

The self-proclaimed first lady of the American theater, Barrymore made her final film appearance in 1957's *Johnny Trouble*, after which she retired from Hollywood. On June 18, 1959, Barrymore died in her sleep at her luxurious Beverly Hills home from a heart attack. Her funeral service was attended by over 200 mourners at the Church of the Good Shepherd in Beverly Hills. Notable attendees were actress Irene Dunne and actor Joseph Cotton.

Ethel Barrymore, 1879-1959.
Courtesy of the Library of Congress (LC-USZ62-103733 DLC)

Ethel Barrymore is interred not far from her brother, Lionel, in the main mausoleum at Calvary Cemetery in Los Angeles, block 60, crypt 3F.

Leo McCarey

Best director Leo McCarey's life and career achievements have been discussed in Chapter two.

Ethel Barrymore's crypt at Calvary Catholic Cemetery.

The Eighteenth Academy Awards
"Calling in Sick"

With World War II over, the awards ceremony returned to the glitz and glamour of years past. It was held on March 7, 1946, at Grauman's Chinese Theater for the third consecutive year and Bob Hope shared the hosting responsibilities with actor James Stewart. Bing Crosby was nominated for a best actor Oscar for a second year in a row, reprising the role of father O'Malley in *The Bells of St. Mary's* (1945), but he did not think he'd win the award and did not bother to show up for the ceremony. Also best actress nominee and eventual winner, Joan Crawford suspiciously came down with the flu the night of the event and did not attend. In reality, the starlet was so nervous, she decided it was better to stay away than be disappointed. The best picture of the year went to Billy Wilder's *The Lost Weekend* (1945), a glimpse into the desperate and haunting life of an alcoholic aspiring writer (played by Ray Milland).

Nominees and Winners

Best Actor
Bing Crosby, Gene Kelly, **Ray Milland**, Gregory Peck, and Cornel Wilde

Best Actress
Ingrid Bergman, **Joan Crawford**, Greer Garson, Jennifer Jones, Gene Tierney

Best Supporting Actor
Michael Chekhov, James Dall, **James Dunn**, Robert Mitchum, and J. Carrol Naish

Best Supporting Actress
Eve Arden, Ann Blyth, Angela Lansbury, Joan Lorring, and **Anne Revere**

Best Director
Clarence Brown, Alfred Hitchcock, Leo McCarey, Jean Renoir, and **Billy Wilder**

Ray Milland
(January 3, 1905 – March 10, 1986)

The charming, but very private and introspective, actor was born Reginald Alfred John Truscott-Jones on January 3, 1905, in Neath, Wales, England. The Welsh-born actor often played the suave and romantic leading man during his prolific film career. He got his break in show business due to an accident in 1929 as a then soldier in the British Calvary; he was chosen to replace an injured actor (who had been hit by a bus) in *The Informer* (1929). The bit part called for a soldier (Milland) to shoot into a target. The producers were so impressed by Milland (he had no previous acting experience) that he was offered another role in *The Flying Scotsman* (1929) and this led to a contract with MGM Studios and his Hollywood career was off and running.

During an award-winning film career that spanned five decades (1929-1985), Milland appeared in over 170 motion pictures and television programs. Some of his most well-known films are:

- *The Bachelor Father* (1931)
- *Bolero* (1934)
- *The Big Broadcast of 1937* (1936)
- *Beau Geste* (1939)

Ray Milland,
1905-1986.

- *Reap the Wild Wind* (1942)
- *The Uninvited* (1944)
- *The Trouble with Women* (1947)
- *Dial M for Murder* (1954)
- *Premature Burial* (1962)
- *Love Story* (1970)
- *Terror in the Wax Museum* (1973)
- *Escape to Witch Mountain* (1975)

His crowning achievement was in 1946, when he won the Oscar for best lead actor, portraying the alcoholic writer, Don Birnam, in *The Lost Weekend* (1945). Upon accepting his award from Actress Ingrid Bergman, Milland appeared to be nervous and unprepared; he simply nodded, smiled and left the stage without uttering a word. He was the first and last best actor Oscar winner not to utter a single word of acceptance.

He was a notoriously private person and stayed away from the glitz and glamour of Hollywood. He never appeared in the gossip magazines and often preferred to stay home with a good book. In 1984, Milland was diagnosed with lung cancer; he continued to work in film and television right up until his death on March 10, 1986. The veteran actor died in his sleep at the Torrance Memorial Hospital in Torrance, California.

Raymond Milland's remains were cremated and scattered at sea, near Redondo Beach, California.

Joan Crawford

(March 23, 1905 – May 10, 1977)

"If you're going to be a star, you have to look like a star, and I never go out unless I look like Joan Crawford, the movie star. If you want to see the girl next door, go next door."

~Joan Crawford

One of Hollywood's most brilliant, unforgettable, and notoriously fickle actresses was born Lucille Fay LeSueur on March 23, 1905 (some sources have the year as 1908), in San Antonio, Texas. Her parents divorced when she was very young. She and her mother then lived a transient lifestyle moving from city to city in the Midwest. Crawford did attend private school, but unfortunately did not progress pass a sixth grade education. She was a talented dancer and always dreamed of becoming an entertainer. As a teenager, she was able to land employment as a chorus girl in Kansas City, Chicago, and Detroit. In 1924, during one of these shows, Crawford was discovered by stage producer J.J. Shubert; he offered her a part in the chorus line of his Broadway play, *Innocent Eyes*. After several months of success in this play, Crawford was spotted by a MGM talent scout; she was offered a screen test and then was offered a bit part in the film, *Pretty Ladies* (1925). After several other small film roles, MGM suggested that she change her name; a public contest was held and Joan Crawford was selected. Initially, she hated the name wanting Joan to be pronounced, Jo-Anne, and thinking that Crawford sounded like crawfish but she had no choice in the matter. Eventually, she grew to embrace the new name and the opportunities she had been given.

In a legendary film career that would span forty-seven years (1925-1972), she would star in over eighty motion pictures. Her most famous film credits include:

- *The Taxi Dancer* (1927)
- *Our Dancing Daughters* (1928)
- *Grand Hotel* (1932)
- *The Bride Wore Red* (1937)
- *The Shining Hour* (1938)
- *The Women* (1939)
- *Humoresque* (1946)
- *Queen Bee* (1955)
- *Autumn Leaves* (1956)
- *The Best of Everything* (1959)

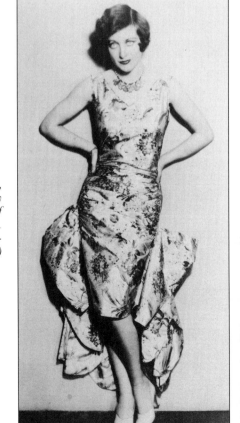

Joan Crawford, circa 1928. *Courtesy of the Library of Congress, George G. Bain Collection (LC-USZ62-133571)*

She won the Oscar for best actress in 1946, for her portrayal of the ambitious mother in *Mildred Pierce* (1945). She was not present at the ceremony because of illness and in a much-staged and somewhat comical scene; she accepted the award from her bed, saying in the most theatrical way possible, "This is the greatest moment of my life." It turned out that she had faked being sick because she was afraid of losing. Crawford was nominated for two further best actress Academy Awards, *Possessed* (1947) and *Sudden Fear* (1952). Her film roles were quite diverse ranging from chorus girls and flappers (1920s), strong minded career woman (1930s and 1940s), and subdued older women (1950s). But by the 1960s, she was relegated to bit parts in B-movies and television appearances. She made a dramatic comeback in the thriller, *What Ever Happened to Baby Jane* (1962) but this revival was short lived, subsequent film roles were unsatisfactory, and she soon retired from film.

She had a very tough persona, notoriously difficult to work with and was always at odds with studio heads. In 1938, she was labeled "box-office poison" by industry insiders. By 1943, MGM studio head Louis B. Mayer had had enough, and fired the actress for refusal to accept roles and abide by her contract. Crawford then signed with Warner Bros. and other studios, where she got roles that were much more to her liking.

Crawford had an infamous ongoing feud with Bette Davis. The two actresses detested one another. Davis was once quoted as saying (about Crawford), "She's slept with every male star at MGM except Lassie," and in return, Crawford replied, "I don't hate Bette Davis even though the press wants me to. I resent her. I don't see how she (Davis) built a career out of a set of mannerisms, instead of real acting ability. Take away the pop eyes, the cigarette, and those funny clipped words and what have you got? She's phony, but I guess the public really likes that." Ironically, the two arch rivals would appear together to revive their careers in 1962's *What Ever Happened to Baby Jane*, Crawford would say that working with Davis in this motion picture was the greatest challenge of her career.

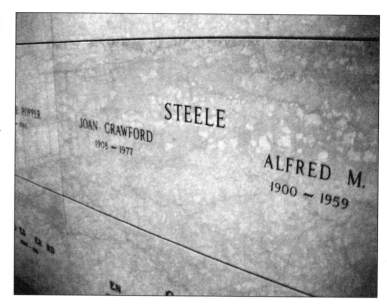

Joan Crawford's crypt at Ferncliff Cemetery.

Her personal life was filled with heartache and turmoil. She married five times, divorced four husbands, and adopted four children, one of which, Christina, wrote a tell-all biography, "Mommie Dearest," in which Crawford was portrayed as being neurotic, obsessive, and abusive. Because she saw this book as the ultimate betrayal, Crawford left her daughter completely out of her will and in the last paragraph of this infamous will, Crawford wrote, "It is my intention to make no provision herein for my son Christopher or my daughter Christina for reasons which are well known to them." In 1955, Crawford married Pepsi Cola Company Chief Executive, Alfred Steele; she became a goodwill ambassador for the company and traveled around the globe promoting Pepsi. When Steele died in 1959, she was elected to fill his spot on the board of directors and held this position until 1973, when she was forced out.

Due to her advancing age and ill health, the last years of her life were spent secluded in her upper Eastside Manhattan, New York, apartment. On May 10, 1977, Crawford died from a heart attack. She had been suffering from pancreatic cancer and was in a weakened state at the time of her death. Crawford's alleged last words, spoken to her housekeeper (who had begun to pray out loud) were "Damin it! Don't you dare ask God to help me." Upon hearing of the death of her long time rival, Bette Davis is said to have remarked "You should never say bad things about the dead; you should only say good things…Joan Crawford is dead. Good."

Crawford was a devote Christian Scientist and her remains were cremated, a brief service was held on May 13, 1977, in which 150 friends and family attended. A memorial service was held at the All Souls Unitarian

Did You Know?

Crawford had a cleanliness obsession. She would often wipe her hands every ten minutes, and follow guests around her house cleaning door knobs and wiping down everything they touched. She always slept in white pajamas and never smoked a cigarette unless she had opened the pack herself. Crawford was once quoted as saying, "I need sex for a clear complexion, but I'd rather do it for love."

Church in New York on May 16th; in attendance were many Hollywood dignitaries that included good friend actress, Myrna Loy.

Crawford's ashes are interred with that of her late husband, Alfred Steele, in the family crypt at the Ferncliff Cemetery mausoleum, Westchester County, Hartsdale, New York, unit 8, alcove E, crypt 42.

James Dunn

(November 2, 1901 – September 3, 1967)

The award winning character actor was born November 2, 1901, in New York City. He worked in vaudeville (as a song and dance man), the theater, and as an extra in several silent films before being signed to a movie contract with 20th Century-Fox studios in 1931. Known for his boy-next-door roles, Dunn's film and television career spanned nearly four decades (1929-1967) and included over fifty feature motion pictures.

In 1946, he won the best supporting Oscar for his portrayal of the drunken waiter, Johnny Nolan, in *A Tree Grows in Brooklyn* (1945). His other notable film credits include:

- *Society Girl* (1932)
- *Take a Chance* (1933)
- *Mysterious Crossing* (1936)
- *Killer McCoy* (1947)

He also starred alongside Shirley Temple in her first three films, *Stand Up and Cheer* (1934), *Baby Take a Bow* (1934), and *Bright Eyes* (1934). In 1950, Dunn retired from motion pictures and began to work exclusively in television and he became one the first Hollywood film actors to star in his own television series, *It's a Great Life* (1954-56). On September 3, 1967, Dunn died at the Santa Monica Hospital after undergoing abdominal surgery.

James Dunn's remains were cremated and the ashes were scattered in the Pacific Ocean.

Anne Revere

(June 25, 1903 – December 18, 1990)

The versatile veteran character actress was born on June 25, 1903, in New York City. She was a graduate of Wellesley College and is a direct descendant of American Revolutionary hero, Paul Revere. She began her show business career on the Broadway stage and graduated to film in 1934's *Double Door*. During her film career (1934-1977), which included nearly forty motion pictures, she often played the role of the strong, maternal figure. Her major film credits include:

- *Men of Boys Town* (1941)
- *Remember the Day* (1941)
- *A Place in the Sun* (1951)

She won the 1946 Oscar for best supporting actress in *National Velvet* (1945), and was nominated for the same award for *The Song of Bernadette* (1943) and *Gentlemen's Agreement* (1947).

In 1947, a year after winning the Oscar, she refused to testify before the U.S. House of Representatives Committee on Un-American Activities, was blacklisted and did not appear in another motion picture for twenty years. Unable to find work in films, she returned to the Broadway stage, where in 1961, she won a Tony Award for her performance in *Toys in the Attic*. She also made numerous television appearances during this period and her last role was in the soap opera, *Ryan's Hope* (1977). Anne Revere died on December 18, 1990, at her home on Long Island, New York, from pneumonia.

Anne Revere's final resting place is at the Mount Auburn Cemetery, Cambridge, Massachusetts, in lot 11002, azalea garden wall.

Billy Wilder

(June 22, 1906 – March 27, 2002)

"The smartest, most gifted people in the world live in Hollywood. Those who knock the town; 1. Never made it, 2. Have no chance to make it, 3. Made it and blew it."
~Billy Wilder

The multi-talented award-winning director, producer, and writer was born Samuel Wilder on June 22, 1906, in Sucha, Austria-Hungry (now Poland). His first foray into show business came at the end of a pen as a screenwriter for UFA studios, one of Germany's top movie producers of the 1920s. He remained in high demand as a writer in Germany, but eventually fled the country in 1933, when Adolf Hitler took power. Sensing that dangerous times were ahead, he first moved to Vienna, then Paris. It was while in France that Wilder wrote a screen play for Columbia Pictures and his American film career was launched. Arriving in Hollywood in 1934, he was unable to speak English and soon found himself out of work and money. Sharing a room with actor Peter Lorre, Wilder taught himself English by watching baseball games and movies. In 1936, he landed a job as a writer for Paramount Studios and was paired with fellow writer Charles Brackett. The pair of Wilder and Brackett would produce fourteen consecutive hit movies.

Did You Know?

Wilder once told actor Billy Bob Thornton that he was too ugly to be an actor and that he should write his own screenplay for himself in which he could exploit his less than perfect features. Thornton followed this advice by writing and starring in *Sling Blade* (1996), for which he won a best screenplay Oscar in 1997.

In a film career that would span four decades (1936-1981), Wilder would write over seventy screen plays, direct twenty-seven feature motion pictures, and produce dozens of other films. His directorial career highlights include:

- *Ninotchka* (1939)
- *Hold Back the Dawn* (1941)
- *Ball of Fury* (1941)
- *The Major and the Minor* (1942)

- *Double Indemnity* (1944)
- *The Emperor Waltz* (1948)
- *A Foreign Affair* (1948)
- *Ace in the Hole* (1951)
- *Stalag 17* (1953)
- *Sabrina* (1954)
- *The Seven Year Itch* (1955)
- *Witness for the Prosecution* (1957)
- *The Spirit of St. Louis* (1957)
- *Some Like It Hot* (1959)
- *The Fortune Cookie* (1966)
- *The Front Page* (1974)

One of the most successful film writer/directors in Hollywood history, Wilder was nominated for twelve best writing and eight best directing Oscars. He won both awards in 1946 for *The Lost Weekend* (1945) and repeated the double victory again in 1961 for *The Apartment* (1960). Wilder also won for best writing in 1951 for *Sunset Boulevard* (1950). The acclaimed director died on March 27, 2002, from pneumonia at his Beverly Hills home. He had been in failing health for a few years prior to his death.

Wilder is buried at Westwood Memorial Park, Los Angeles, in the chapel estates section near actors Carroll O'Conner and Walter Mathau. His tombstone epitaph reads, "I'm a writer but then nobody's perfect."

Director Billy Wilder's grave at Westwood Memorial Park.

The Nineteenth Academy Awards Ceremony
"Feuding Sisters Part Two"

The award ceremony moved from the somewhat intimate Grauman's Chinese Theater to the immense 6,000 plus seat, Shrine Auditorium. It was held on March 13, 1947, and hosted by Jack Benny; at the event many of the well-known invitees got the "Oscar flu," and did not attend, including Bing Crosby, Frank Sinatra, Judy Garland, and Joan Crawford. The rift between sisters Olivia de Havilland and Joan Fontaine had been a well known fact for years, ever since Fontaine won the best actress statuette in 1941 (de Havilland thought she deserved the award). The rivalry heated up when Fontaine was chosen to present the best actress Oscar, Joan Crawford was ill again and could not attend. An awkward niceness prevailed on stage between the battling sisters when Olivia won the award, but all niceties were dropped backstage when Fontaine extended a hand of congratulations to her sister. Olivia promptly rebuffed the congratulatory handshake. The best picture of the year went to Billy Wilder's, *The Best Years of Our Lives* (1946), a drama about returning World War II veterans.

Nominees and Winners

Best Actor
Fredric March, Laurence Olivier, Larry Parks, Gregory Peck, and James Stewart

Best Actress
Jane Wyman, Rosalind Russell, **Olivia de Havilland**, Celia Johnson, and Jennifer Jones

Best Supporting Actor
Charles Coburn, William Demarest, Claude Rains, **Harold Russell**, and Clifton Webb

Best Supporting Actress
Ethel Barrymore, **Anne Baxter**, Lillian Gish, Flora Robson, and Gale Sondergaard

Best Director
Clarence Brown, Frank Capra, David Lean, Robert Siodmak, and **William Wyler**

Fredric March

Best lead actor winner for 1946, Fredric March's life and accomplishments are discussed in chapter two.

Olivia de Havilland
(Born July 1, 1916 in Tokyo, Japan)

Olivia de Havilland, the last surviving lead character from 1939's *Gone With the Wind*, and the 1946 winner of the best lead actress Oscar for *To Each His Own*, was born on July 1, 1916 in Tokyo, Japan and currently resides in Paris, France.

Harold Russell
(January 14, 1914 – January 29, 2002)

The best supporting Oscar winner for 1947 was not even a professional actor. Harold John Russell was born on January 14, 1914, in North Sydney, Nova Scotia and raised in Cambridge, Massachusetts. He joined the Army on December 8, 1941, the day after the bombing of Pearl Harbor and became a paratrooper and explosives expert. In 1944, at Fort Mackall, North Carolina, he had a charge of TNT explode in his hands during a training exercise. The injuries were so extensive that both hands hand to be amputated. A short time after the accident, he was cast in an Army documentary, *Diary of a Sergeant* that detailed his rehabilitation efforts. Hollywood film director, William Wyler saw this documentary and offered Russell the part of Homer Parish in *The Best Years of Our Lives* (1946). His performance in this film was critically and commercially well received, and he was nominated for a best supporting Academy. He beat out other veteran actors to win the award. Upon accepting the gold statuette, Russell was so moved by the rousing applause from the audience that he was overcome with emotion and reduced to tears. He also received an honorary Oscar, "For bringing hope and courage to his fellow veterans through his appearance in The Best Years of Our Lives." He is the only actor to ever receive two Oscars for the same role.

Anne Baxter

(May 7, 1923 – December 12, 1985)

Following this film, Russell attended Brown University and then became a founder member of AMVETS. He also made it his lifelong quest to help the disabled. He went on to appear in a handful of films and several television programs such as *Inside Moves* (1980), *Trapper John, M.D.* (1981), and *Dogtown* (1997). Russell wrote two autobiographies, *Victory in My Hands* (1947) and *The Best Years of My Life* (1981). In 1992, Russell caused a stir when he decided to sell his best supporting actor Oscar. Russell told the press that he wanted put some money away for his children and grandchildren. The Academy of Motion Pictures Sciences urged him not sell and even tried to purchase the statuette, offering $20,000 but Russell held out and it was eventually sold for more than $60,000 to an anonymous buyer. On January 29, 2002, Russell died from a heart attack at age eighty-eight.

Harold Russell's grave is found at the Lakeview Cemetery in Cochituate, Massachusetts.

The multitalented Academy Award winning actress was born on May 7, 1923, in Michigan City, Indiana, but grew up in Bronxville, New York. In 1936, at the age of thirteen, Baxter made her Broadway theater debut in *Seen But Not Heard*, garnering rave reviews, but she yearned for Hollywood's bright lights. An initial foray into film in 1937 was unsuccessful and Baxter returned to Broadway. Then in 1940, at age seventeen, she was given another chance, was given a screen test at 20th Century Fox Studios, and was offered a seven year movie contract. Before she could make a movie for Fox, she was loaned out to MGM where she appeared in *20 Mule Team* (1940). Her early film career was filled with great success and roles that other actresses would have had to work for years to attain. She was an actress who relied on her charm rather than great beauty and would star in over fifty motion pictures and numerous television series from 1940 to 1985; her film credits include:

- *The Pied Piper* (1942)
- *The North Star* (1943)
- *Angel on My Shoulder* (1946)
- *The Walls of Jericho* (1948)
- *Follow the Sun* (1951)
- *Cimarron* (1960)

She won the best supporting actress Oscar in 1947 for *The Razor's Edge* (1946) and was nominated in 1951 for *All About Eve* (1950). Perhaps her most famous role is that of the beautiful and conniving Queen Nefretiri in Cecile B. DeMille's *The Ten Commandments* (1956).

Anne Baxter, 1923-1985.

In 1960, tiring of the bright lights and glamour of Hollywood, she retired from film and settled with her second husband, Randolph Galt, on a cattle ranch in Australia. In 1970, after a decade away from show business, she yearned to return to the screen saying, "Acting is not what I do. It's what I am. It is my permanent, built-in cathedral." She then became a staple of television appearing in numerous programs such as *East of Eden* (1981) and *Hotel* (1983). Her last appearance was in the made-for-television movie, *The Masks of Death* (1984). On December 8, 1985, while walking along Madison Avenue in Manhattan, she collapsed from a stroke. Baxter was rushed to Lenox Hill Hospital, where she lay in a coma for eight days. She died on December 12, 1985, never regaining consciousness.

Anne Baxter's cremated remains are interred at the Lloyd-Jones Cemetery next to the historic Unity Chapel in Spring Green, Wisconsin. Her ashes rest under a small tree memorial which is marked by a nondescript marker. It is near the now-empty gravesite of her famous grandfather (Frank Lloyd Wright's remains were disinterred and moved to Scottsdale, Arizona in the mid-1980s). The cemetery is situated in the valley not far from Wright's historic Taliesin estate.

Anne Baxter's grave marker.

The Lloyd-Jones Cemetery, Baxter's memorial tree and final resting place are pictured in the foreground, Frank Lloyd Wright's former burial site is seen in the far left, the Unity Chapel to the right in the background.

William Wyler

Best Director William Wyler's life story and career achievements have been discussed earlier in this chapter.

Actress Anne Baxter with her Grandfather, famed architect Frank Lloyd Wright. *Courtesy of the Herald Examiner Collection/ Los Angeles Public Library*

The Twentieth Academy Awards Ceremony
"A Very Youthful Surprise"

On a very chilly thirty degree night in Los Angeles, the Academy of Motion Picture Arts and Sciences handed out its awards for film achievement from 1947. The event was held on March 20, 1948, at the Shrine Auditorium and was hosted by actor Dick Powell and actress Agnes Moorehead. For the first time in many years, notorious "no show" Joan Crawford, made a rare appearance at the event, she was again nominated for a best actress Oscar. The night was filled with few surprises, but one huge upset in the best actress race sent the audience into a tizzy. Front-runner Rosalind Russell was the favorite to win the gold statuette for her performance in *Mourning Becomes Electra* (1947). With only one award left to present (best actress) and with the outcome a perceived forgone conclusion; many in the audience began to find the exits. As presenter Fredric March tore open the envelope, he did a double take. Loretta Young had won. As he announced Young's name, the surprised crowd stopped in their tracks. A truly stunned Loretta Young rushed to the stage to accept the award and double checked the envelope, just to make sure she had actually won. Rarely had a bigger upset occurred in the twenty year history of the Oscars. The best picture of the year was awarded to Darryl F. Zanuck's, *Gentleman's Agreement* (1947).

Did You Know?
The movie *Crossfire* (1947) was the first "B" movie to be nominated for a best picture Oscar.

Nominees and Winners

Best Actor
Michael Redgrave, **Ronald Colman**, John Garfield, Gregory Peck, and William Powell

Best Actress
Joan Crawford, Susan Hayward, Dorothy McGuire, Rosalind Russell, and **Loretta Young**

Best Supporting Actor
Charles Bickford, Thomas Gomez, **Edmund Gwenn**, Robert Ryan, and Richard Widmark

Best Supporting Actress
Ethel Barrymore, Gloria Grahame, **Celeste Holm**, Marjorie Main, and Anne Revere

Best Director
George Cukor, Edward Dmytryk, **Elia Kazan**, Henry Koster, and David Lean

Ronald Colman
(February 9, 1891 – May 19, 1958)

[To his agent] *"Before God I'm worth 35 dollars a week. Before the motion picture industry I'm worth anything you can get."*
~Ronald Colman

Ronald Colman, 1891-1958.

The esteemed British actor was born on February 9, 1891, in Richmond, Surrey, England. A veteran of the First World War, Colman gravitated to the English theater and vaudeville circuit. Feeling that America held more opportunities for an actor, he arrived in New York City in 1920. Virtually penniless, and after two years of struggles, Colman got his big break as a supporting actor in the Broadway hit, *La Tendresse*. Motion picture director, Henry King saw Colman and cast him alongside Lillian Gish in *The White Sister* (1923). Colman was an immediate hit in film, becoming one of Hollywood's greatest romantic leading men. In a film and television career that spanned thirty-four years (1923-1957), Colman appeared in over forty feature motion pictures. His greatest film credits include:

- *The Dark Angel* (1925)
- *Kiki* (1926)
- *The Night of Love* (1927)
- *The Rescue* (1929)
- *Arrowsmith* (1931)
- *A Tale of Two Cities* (1935)
- *Lost Horizon* (1937)
- *The Prisoner of Zenda* (1937)
- *Kismet* (1944)

Due to his smooth and cultivated voice, he was able to successfully cross the barrier from silent film to talking pictures and became one of the greatest actors of the golden age.

In 1930, he was nominated for two best acting Oscars for *Condemned* (1929) and *Bulldog Drummond* (1929). He was nominated again in 1943 for the best acting honors for his portrayal of Smithy in *Random Harvest* (1942). In his third attempt at Oscar gold, Colman finally took home the coveted statuette for *A Double Life* (1947). After this award-winning performance in 1947, Colman made only one more full-length film, 1950's *Champagne for Caesar*. He instead focused on *The Halls of Ivy*, a radio show and later a television program of the same name.

Colman had a dislike for the Hollywood lifestyle and near the end of his life retired to his ranch in San Ysidro, California. He was married for twenty years to actress Benita Hume. On May 19, 1958, the veteran actor died at St. Francis Hospital in Santa Barbara, California, from pneumonia. Fibrosis of the lungs and pneumonia plagued the actor most of his adult life. While serving in the British armed forces during World War I, he contacted the illness and never fully recovered. His funeral service was held at the All Saints Episcopal Church in Montecito, California. More than 200 mourners were in attendance for the short service (only fourteen minutes). Among the Hollywood dignitaries present were long-time friend William Powell, Jack Benny, Vincent Price, Joseph Cotton, and George Sanders. Ironically, less than nine months after Colman's death, Sanders would marry his widow Benita Hume.

Colman's remains were cremated and buried at the Santa Barbara Cemetery in the Ridge lawn section. His tombstone epitaph reads in part "Our revels are now ended. These our actors. As I foretold you. Were all spirits. And are melted into air. Into thin air. We are all such stuff as dreams are made on. And our little life is rounded with sleep."

Ronald Colman's grave at the Santa Barbara Cemetery.

Loretta Young

(January 6, 1913 – August 12, 2000)

*"In 1949, there was a new thing called television, to which
my agency and advisors opposed as a performance medium."*

~Loretta Young

The elegant award-winning actress, whose on-screen image as the wholesome girl next door brought tremendous success in Hollywood was born Gretchen Michaela Young on January 6, 1913, in Salt Lake City, Utah. Her parents were separated when Loretta was three years old when the family moved to Southern California. Needing money, Loretta's mother allowed the youngster to act in order to raise some cash for the family. Loretta's first motion picture was 1919's, *The Only Way;* in this film she played the small part of a crying child on an operating table. Loretta was very ambitious and strove for excellence on screen even in the early years of her film career. She was candid about wanting fame and stardom, not wanting to be just an actress.

In a film and television career that spanned seven decades (1919 to 1994), she appeared in 100 motion pictures. She played opposite all of the major romantic leading men of the era, including Clark Gable, Gary Cooper, Tyrone Power, Spencer Tracy, and James Cagney. She made an easy transition from silent film to talkies, and with her ever-youthful appearance and wholesome image, delighted film going audiences year after year.

Young's major film credits include:

- *The Sheik* (1921)
- *The Magnificent Flirt* (1928)
- *The Head Man* (1928)
- *Kismet* (1930)
- *Life Begins* (1932)
- *They Call it Sin* (1932)
- *The Life of Jimmy Dolan* (1933)
- *Born to be Bad* (1934)
- *Shanghai* (1935)
- *The Call of the Wild* (1935)
- *Ramona* (1936)
- *Kentucky* (1938)
- *Ladies Courageous* (1944)
- *The Bishop's* Wife (1947)
- *It Happens Every Thursday* (1953)

In 1948, in a shocking upset, Young won the best actress Oscar for her portrayal of the witty Swedish maid-turned-Congresswoman, Katrin Holstrom, in *The Farmer's Daughter* (1947). Young was nominated for a second best actress Academy Award in 1950 for *Come to the Stable* (1949), but lost to Olivia de Havilland.

Loretta Young, 1913-2000.

While Young was very protective of her wholesome on-screen image, she was hard pressed to keep that image off screen. The many contradictions in her public and private life were exemplified by an early marriage (at age 17) that ended in divorce, and carried on numerous love affairs with many of her male co-stars, most notably Clark Gable with whom she co-starred with in 1935's *The Call of the Wild*. This affair allegedly produced an illegitimate daughter (Judy Lewis) who was subsequently reported as being adopted. It has been noted that Judy was the right age to have been born during Young's mysterious sojourn to Europe following filming of *The Crusades* in 1935 and that Judy's uncanny resemblance to Gable is remarkable. To her dying day, Young remained coy and denied these allegations but left a tantalizing quote in the book *Hollywood Royalty* (1992), "Clark Gable certainly was everything that he appeared to be."

Did You Know?

Legendary actress Marlene Dietrich (no stranger to scandal herself) was quoted as saying, "Every time she (Loretta Young) sins, she builds a church. That's why there are so many Catholic churches in Hollywood." Young is the godmother to actress Marlo Thomas and the late Michael Wayne (the son of actor John Wayne).

In the early 1950s, as her film career began to wane, Young took a gamble and ventured into television. Her move to the small screen was roundly criticized but she was determined to try anyway. On September 20, 1953, *A Letter to Loretta* (AKA, *The Loretta Young Show*) aired on NBC and had a successful eight-year run. The remainder of her life was filled with philanthropic ventures. She wrote a book in 1961 entitled, *The Things I Had to Learn*, and made occasional forays into television. On August 12, 2000, Young died from ovarian cancer at the Los Angeles home of her sister Georgiana Montalban (wife of actor Ricardo Montalban). Her funeral service was held at the St. Louis Catholic Church in Cathedral City, California.

Loretta Young is buried at Holy Cross Catholic Cemetery, Culver City, California in section F, tier 65, space 49. Young's grave is unmarked and she is interred within the same plot as her mother, Gladys Belzer.

Loretta Young's final resting place at Holy Cross Catholic Cemetery.

Edmund Gwenn

(September 26, 1877 – September 6, 1959)

The venerable character actor, who will forever be known for his portrayal of Kris Kringle was born Edmund Kellaway on September 26, 1877, in Wandsworth, London, England. His parents disapproved of his interest in the theater and disowned him when at seventeen, he chose an acting career rather than a civil service profession. They were reconciled many years later when Gwenn neared his acting peak. At the age of twenty in a chance meeting, he was introduced to famed playwright George Bernard Shaw. The famed playwright offered the young actor a prominent role in his London production of *Man and Superman*. Gwenn's performance was critically acclaimed, and this led to five other Shaw stage productions. At the outbreak of World War I, Gwenn enlisted in the British Army and eventually rose to the rank of captain. Following the war, he resumed his London stage acting career, eventually moving to New York City and the bright lights of Broadway. Gwenn was a success here as well, appearing in numerous stage productions. His prolific motion picture career began in 1931 with *How He Lied to Her Husband* and from there on out, Gwenn was devoted primarily to film. During a screen and television career that spanned two decades (1931- 1957), he appeared in over eighty feature motion pictures that included:

- *Tell Me Tonight* (1932)
- *Marooned* (1933)
- *Sylvia Scarlett* (1935)
- *Anthony Adverse* (1936)
- *All American Chump* (1936)
- *Pride and Prejudice* (1938)
- *Foreign Correspondent* (1940)
- *The Devil and Miss Jones* (1941)
- *Charley's Aunt* (1941)
- *Lassie Come Home* (1943)
- *Of Human Bondage* (1946)
- *Hills of Home* (1948)
- *Bonzo Goes to College* (1952)
- *Them* (1954) [[another favorite of mine!]]

He won the best supporting actor Oscar in 1948 for his portrayal of the loveable Kris Kringle in *Miracle on 34th Street* (1947) and upon accepting his statuette, Gwenn was quoted as saying, "Now, I know there is a Santa Claus." He was again nominated for a best supporting actor Academy Award in 1951 for *Mister 880* (1950), but lost to George Sanders.

Late in life, Gwenn was crippled by severe arthritis and this ended his film career. Gwenn's final days were spent in tremendous pain at the Motion Picture and Television Actors Home in Woodland Hills. He suffered a stroke and later developed pneumonia and died on September 6, 1959. A memorial service was held at the Motion Picture and Television Actors Home and at the All Saints Episcopal Church in Beverly Hills.

Edmund Gwenn's cremated remains are interred at the Chapel of the Pines Crematory in Los Angeles.

Edmund Gwenn, 1877-1959.

Celeste Holm

A multi-talented actress of film, stage, and television, Celeste Holm was born on April 29, 1917, in New York City. She made her first major Broadway appearance in 1940 with *The Time of Your Life*, co-starring Gene Kelly. Holm was signed by 20th Century Fox in 1946 and her first screen role was in *Three Little Girls in Blue*. In her third film, *Gentleman's Agreement* (1947), she would win the best supporting actress Academy Award and Golden Globe. She would be nominated for two additional Oscars for *Come to the Stable* (1949) and *All About Eve* (1950).

[Commenting on Bette Davis] *"I walked onto the set of* All About Eve *on the first day and said, "Good morning, and do you know her reply? She said, 'Oh shit, good manners.' I never spoke to her again—ever."*

~Celeste Holm

"Professionally she found Ms. Davis to be a consummate professional and years later Bette did come back stage to congratulate her on her current success and new Broadway show."

~Frank Basile (Celeste's Husband)

Holm's true love has always been the stage and by the mid-1950s, she had basically left Hollywood for the brighter lights of Broadway. In 1954, Holm appeared in her own television series, *Honestly Celeste* (1954). In 1979, she was nominated for two Emmy Awards and another in 1987. Holm has remained very active and has made numerous stage, film, and television appearances. She presently resides in New York City with her husband, renowned opera singer, Frank Basile.

Celeste Holm presenting Walter Huston with his "Best Supporting Actor" Oscar at the 21st Academy Awards Ceremony, March 24, 1949.
Courtesy of the Los Angeles Public Library Collection.

Elia Kazan

(September 7, 1909 – September 28, 2003)

"When you know what an actor has, you can reach in and arouse it. If you don't know what he has, you don't know what the hell is going on."

~Elia Kazan

Elia Kazan was one of the giants of American film; he was respected by many and despised by others. He was born Elias Kazanjoglou on September 7, 1909, in Constantinople, Turkey. Kazan immigrated to the United States in his late teens to attend college at Williams College, Williamstown, Massachusetts, and after graduation studied drama at Yale University. In 1932, he joined the Group Theater in New York City, there he met and became good friends with Lee Strasberg. This group evolved and began to advocate for social change through political agitation. It was during this time that Kazan joined the Communist Party and embraced left-wing politics, which had become popular among the theater crowd. After two years he became disenchanted with the party and left the organization but he continued to be an advocate of free speech and discussion.

In the early 1940s, Kazan arrived in Hollywood, first appearing as an actor in a few forgettable films, then finding his true calling behind the camera. His directorial debut came in 1945 with *A Tree Grows in Brooklyn*, and although he would only direct twenty feature motion pictures in career that spanned three decades (1945-1976), he would make some of Hollywood's greatest films that include:

- *Boomerang!* (1947)
- *Man on a Tightrope* (1953)
- *Baby Doll* (1956)
- *Wild River* (1960)
- *Splendor in the Grass* (1961)
- *The Arrangement* (1969)
- *The Last Tycoon* (1976)

Kazan was nominated for five best director Academy Awards, winning twice, his Oscar nominated films were:

- *A Street Car Named Desire* (1951)
- *East of Eden* (1955)
- *America, America* (1963)

Kazan's directorial award winning movies were:

- *Gentlemen's Agreement* (1947)
- *On The Waterfront* (1954)

Kazan's films were moody and realistic; they were filled with drama that dealt with American problems and the characters in these movies were often absorbed with intensity. He was a proponent of the method acting style and in 1947 cofounded the legendary Actors Studio in New York City.

In the mid-1950s, Kazan became entangled in the House Un-American Activities Commission hearings. He felt pressured by the committee to name Communists in the film industry and because of this was labeled a pariah by many in Hollywood. Unapologetic, Kazan forged on and in his 1954 Oscar-winning film, *On the Waterfront*, Kazan's unrepentant attitude towards ratting out former friends and colleagues resonates. In a critical scene from the movie, actor Marlon Brando's character shouts, "I'm glad what I done—you hear me?—Glad what I done!" Kazan later said that the dialogue in this film was meant to convey a message, a message that he was glad to have testified the way he did and that he had no regrets.

Kazan went on to have great successes both in movies and Broadway, and in 1999 received an honorary Academy Award for lifetime achievement. On September 28, 2003, Elia Kazan died from natural causes at his home in New York City.

Elia Kazan's burial location is unknown.

The Twenty-First Academy Awards Ceremony
"Feeling Left Out"

This year's event honoring film achievement from 1948 was moved from the huge Shrine Auditorium to the very intimate Academy Awards Theater in West Hollywood (the address was 9038 Melrose Avenue and the building has since been razed) because of a recent Supreme Court ruling on theater monopolies. But in reality, there was a more threatening reason for the move; the major studios were furious with the increasing number of foreign nominated films and pulled the plug on financing the ceremony. The Academy board had to scramble with a small budget and decided on the intimate 900-seat theater; the venue was not big enough to hold all of the Academy members and there were many hurt feelings, but the event was held anyway on March 24, 1949. The host was actor George Montgomery. The first tandem of father and son Oscar winners, John and Walter Huston won for director and best supporting actor in *The Treasure of the Sierra Madre* (1948), the best picture of the year went to *Hamlet* (1948), which was the first non-Hollywood made film to win the honors.

The Nominees and Winners

Best Actor
Lew Ayres, Montgomery Clift, Dan Dailey, **Laurence Olivier**, and Clifton Webb

Best Actress
Ingrid Bergman, Olivia de Havilland, Irene Dunne, Barbara Stanwyck, and **Jane Wyman**

Best Supporting Actor
Charles Bickford, Jose Ferrer, Oscar Homolka, **Walter Huston**, and Cecil Kellaway

Best Supporting Actress
Barbara Bel Geddes, Ellen Corby, Agnes Moorehead, Jean Simmons, and **Claire Trevor**

Best Director
John Huston, Anatole Litvak, Jean Negulesco, Laurence Olivier, and Fred Zinnemann

Laurence Olivier
(May 22, 1907 – July 11, 1989)

"You need to be a bit of a bastard to be a star."
~Laurence Olivier

He was considered by many to be the greatest actor of his time and a living reincarnation of the traditional Shakespearian thespians of times long past; Sir Laurence Kerr Olivier was born on May 22, 1907, in Dorking, Surrey, England. The youngest of three children, Olivier was raised in a very strict religious home. His father was a high-ranking Anglican priest and his mother, while tender and doting, died when Laurence was only twelve. Laurence's Uncle Sydney Olivier was the first Baron Olivier and was Governor of Jamaica and Secretary of State for India.

His love for acting began at an early age, performing in school plays. Because of his natural talent for the performing arts, his father agreed to support this calling. While a student at the Central School of Speech and Drama in London, he appeared in numerous Shakespearian productions and his roles became more and more significant. Moving to New York City in the late 1920s, Olivier's star status rapidly gained momentum and soon caught the eye of Hollywood studio executives. His first foray into film came in 1930 with *The Temporary Widow* and his first starring role came the next year in *The Yellow Ticket* (1931); Olivier, however, did not hold either of these films in high regard. Although his greatest successes were to come on the silver screen, he always held contempt for the medium; his first love would always be the stage.

In a show business career that would span nearly six decades (1930-1989), Olivier would appear in over eighty feature films and television programs. His greatest film achievements include:

- *Perfect Understanding* (1933)
- *Conquest of the Air* (1936)
- *Pride and Prejudice* (1940)
- *21 Days* (1940)
- *That Hamilton Woman* (1941)
- *The Prince and the Show Girl* (1957)
- *Spartacus* (1960)
- *Khartoum* (1966)
- *Battle of Britain* (1969)
- *Dracula* (1979)
- *The Jazz Singer* (1980)
- *Clash of the Titans* (1981)

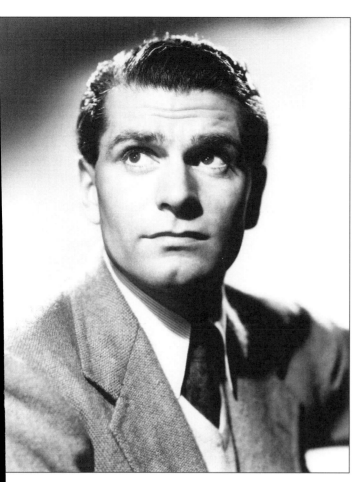

Laurence Olivier, 1907-1989.

He was nominated for eight best acting Oscars:

- *Wuthering Heights* (1939)
- *Rebecca* (1940)
- *The Chronicles History of King Henry V* (1944)
- *Hamlet* (1948)
- *Richard III* (1955)
- *The Entertainer* (1960)
- *Othello* (1965)
- *Sleuth* (1972)
- *The Boys from Brazil* (1978)

Olivier was also nominated for a best director and supporting actor Oscars for *Hamlet* (1948) and *The Marathon Man* (1976), respectively. His only win came in 1949 for his portrayal of the title role of Hamlet, Prince of Denmark, in *Hamlet* (1948). He was also the recipient of two honorary Academy Awards, 1947 for outstanding achievement as an actor, producer, and director for *Henry V* (1946), and 1979 for lifetime achievement in film.

Unlike his professional career, his personal life was filled with turmoil. He was married three times and divorced twice, most notably to fellow Academy Award winning actress Vivien Leigh. Olivier met Leigh while the pair were still married to others and carried on a torrid love affair. They eventually married on August 30, 1940, and their tumultuous union lasted twenty years. Throughout his life, Olivier was known as a notorious womanizer and had numerous affairs which included his second wife, Vivien Leigh, Claire Bloom, and his third wife, Joan Plowright. It has been alleged, but never proven, that he was bi-sexual. Rumors of romantic trysts with fellow actors Danny Kaye and Henry Ainley have persisted but no actual evidence has ever been produced. But in a tantalizing 2006 radio interview, Joan Plowright responded to a question about these rumors by saying, "If a man is touched by genius, he is not an ordinary person. He doesn't lead an ordinary life. He has extremes of behavior which you understand and you just find a way not to be swept overboard by his demons."

Laurence Olivier died on July 11, 1989, at his country home in Steyning, West Sussex, England. The exact cause of his death is in dispute, some sources point to kidney failure and others to complications from a muscle disorder. What is known is that Olivier had been in poor health for many years and just four months prior to his death, the actor had undergone hip replacement surgery after a fall.

Olivier's cremated remains are interred at Westminster Abbey, London, England in Poets Corner, one of only four actors to have been accorded this honor and he is interred ironically near many of the famous people he portrayed both on stage and screen.

Jane Wyman

(January 5, 1917 – September 10, 2007)

[On her refusal to publicly discuss the political career of her ex-husband, Ronald Reagan] *"It's not because I'm bitter or because I don't agree with him politically. I've always been a registered Republican. But it's bad taste to talk about ex-husbands and ex-wives, that's all. Also, I don't know a damn thing about politics."*

~Jane Wyman

Known as a talented and classy actress whose award-winning and distinguished film career was nearly overshadowed by her failed third marriage to actor and future U.S. President Ronald Reagan, Wyman was born Sarah Jane Mayfield on January 5, 1917, in St. Joseph, Missouri. (It must be noted that her actual birth year is in dispute and it has been alleged that she may have been born as many as five years earlier than actually has been published.) Wyman came from a broken home; her parents divorced when she was very young and her father died prematurely.

After high school, with the help of her mother, she attempted to break into show business but early attempts failed. While attending the University of Missouri, she moonlighted as a radio singer under the name of Jane Durrell. She got her start in films in 1932 as a member of the chorus line in *The Kid from Spain*; other yet unknown cast members from this film included Betty Grable and Paulette Goddard. Throughout the early to late 1930s, Wyman appeared in numerous "B" movies as a contract player at Warner Bros. Studios and it was during this time that she met and eventually married actor Ronald Reagan. The pair first appeared on film together in *Brother Rat* (1938) and the two were married on January 26, 1940; they would appear together in three additional motion pictures. Their union lasted eight years, producing one biological daughter (Maureen Reagan) and one adopted son (Michael Reagan), and in 1948 ended in divorce. After Reagan became Governor of California and then President in 1980, Wyman refused to comment on their marriage and considered it bad taste to talk of ex-husbands.

Jane Wyman, 1917-2007.

Professionally, Wyman's film career as a dramatic actress was not taken seriously until after appearing alongside Ray Milland in *The Lost Weekend* (1945). The following year she starred in *The Yearling* (1946) and received a best actress Oscar nomination and in 1949 won Oscar gold as best lead actress for her portrayal of a deaf-mute rape victim in *Johnny Belinda* (1948). This was the first time since the silent movie era that an actress had won the award by not saying a word. There were whispers that Academy voters had given her the Oscar out of sympathy, due to a recent miscarriage and tumultuous divorce from Ronald Reagan. Upon accepting the award, Wyman was quoted as saying, "I accept this very gratefully for keeping my mouth shut for once. I think I will do it again." In following years, she would be nominated twice more for best actress Academy Awards in 1952 for *The Blue Veil* (1951) and 1955 for *Magnificent Obsession* (1954).

Did You Know?
Wyman's divorce from Ronald Reagan was allegedly caused by an affair she had with fellow actor Lew Ayres but she attributed the demise of her marriage to Reagan's incessant and boring discussion of politics. She also holds the record for the longest on-screen movie kiss (three minutes and five seconds) with Regis Toomey in *You're in the Army Now* (1941).

In a film and television career that would span six decades from 1932 to 1993, Wyman would appear in eighty-six motion pictures and numerous television series some of which include:

- *Ready Willing and Able* (1937)
- *The Angel from Texas* (1940)
- *Bad Men of Missouri* (1941)
- *Night and Day* (1946)
- *The Glass Menagerie* (1950)
- *Pollyanna* (1960)

Television credits include:

- *Jane Wyman Presents: The Fireside Theatre* (1955-58
- *Falcon Crest* (1981-1990)

In 1993, she retired from show business and moved to the Palm Springs area; there she remained active as the national chairwoman of the National Arthritis Foundation.

On September 10, 2007, Wyman died from of complications of arthritis and diabetes at her home in Rancho Mirage, California. The actress had been in failing health for several years prior to her death. Her funeral was held at the Sacred Heart Catholic Church in Palm Desert, California.

Jane Wyman is buried at Forest Lawn Memorial Park, Cathedral City in the Mission Santa Rosa outdoor mausoleum, crypt 5F.

Jane Wyman's crypt at Forest Lawn—Cathedral City.

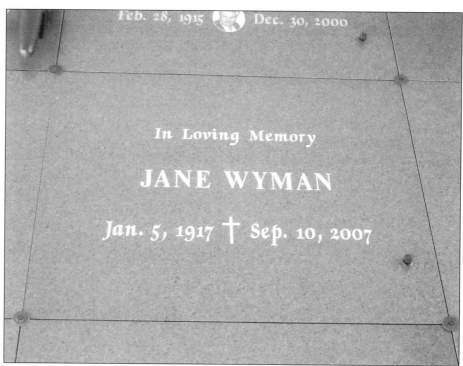

Walter Huston

(April 6, 1884 – April 7, 1950)

The patriarch of the famous Huston acting family, Walter Huston was an accomplished and award-winning character. He was born Walter Houghston on April 6, 1884, in Toronto, Canada. In 1902, at the age of eighteen, Huston ran away from home and joined a traveling theater company, eventually finding himself in New York City, where he found employment in several small stage productions. After a three-year period of little or no stage work, Huston contemplated quitting show business and returning to Toronto. In 1909, Huston again returned to show business as a headliner for the traveling vaudeville act of Whippie and Huston.

Returning to the Broadway stage in the mid-1920s, he had great success, but with the advent of talking pictures, he, like many other actors, chose to travel west to Hollywood in search of stardom. In a film career that spanned two decades (1929-1950), Huston appeared in over fifty motion pictures, most notably:

- *The Virginian* (1929)
- *Abraham Lincoln* (1930)
- *Law and Order* (1932)
- *Of Human Hearts* (1938)
- *The Maltese Falcon* (1941)
- *The North Star* (1943)

He was nominated for two best lead actor Academy Awards in 1937 and 1942 for *Dodsworth* (1936) and *All That Money Can Buy* (1941). In 1943, he was again nominated for an acting Oscar but this time for a best supporting role in *Yankee Doodle Dandy* (1942). In 1949, Huston finally won the coveted statuette for best supporting actor in *The Treasure of the Sierra Madre* (1948). His son, John Huston, won best director honors for the same film and they became the first father-son tandem to win the award. In accepting his award, Walter Huston was quoted as saying, "Many years ago…many, many years ago, I brought up a boy, and I said to him, 'Son, if you ever become a writer, try to write a good part for your old man sometime.' Well, by cranky, that's what he did!"

On April 7, 1950, a little over a year after his big Oscar win and only a day after celebrating his sixty-sixth birthday, Walter Huston died. The actor suffered an aortic aneurysm and peacefully passed away in his sleep. Controversy exists as to whether the actor actually died at the Beverly Hills Hotel or at his home. On April 11, 1950, a memorial service was held at the Academy Theater, the same place where a year earlier he had accepted the Oscar. Numerous Hollywood dignitaries were in attendance including Jimmy Durante, Agnes Moorehead, and Keenan Wynn, and honorary ushers were Humphrey Bogart, John Garfield, Spencer Tracy, and Edward G. Robinson. In his eulogy of the great actor, Spencer Tracy said, "Professionally, he was easy to rate. He was the best."

Some controversy exists as to where Huston's cremated remains were stored from 1950 to 1973. According to author Lawrence Grobel's book, *The Hustons*, Walter's ashes lay unclaimed at a New York City funeral home for twenty three years. Then in 1973, at the death of Nan Sunderland, Walter's widow, John Huston had his father's remains buried at Belmont Memorial Park in Fresno, California in section 8, plot 702, space 2.

Walter Huston, 1884-1950.

Claire Trevor

(March 8, 1910? – April 8, 2000)

The award-winning and versatile actress was one of the most sought-after supporting actresses of the 1930s and 1940s. The blonde and vivacious actress was best known for playing bad girls on screen that included tough-minded molls and floozies. She was born Claire Wemlinger on March 8, 1910, in the borough of Brooklyn, New York. Claire began acting at the age of eleven. She dreamed of becoming a ballerina and loved the stage. She attended Columbia University and the American Academy of Dramatic Arts in New York, but she had to drop out for financial reasons.

Claire made her professional stage debut in 1930 with the Robert Henderson Repertory company and appeared in her first Broadway production in 1932's, *Whistling in the Dark*. In that same year, she was discovered and signed to a contract by 20th Century Fox studios. Her first Hollywood film came in 1933 with the low-budget western, *The Life in the Raw*. In a film and television career that spanned fifty-plus years (1933-1987), Trevor appeared in nearly seventy motion pictures that include:

- *Dante's Inferno* (1935)
- *The Amazing Dr. Clitterhouse* (1938)
- *Street of Chance* (1942)
- *The Woman of the Town* (1943)
- *Murder, My Sweet* (1944)
- *Johnny Angel* (1945)
- *Best of the Badmen* (1951).

Claire Trevor, 1910-2000.

In 1938, she was nominated for her first best supporting actress Academy Award in *Dead End*. The next year, she received top billing in John Ford's iconic western, *Stagecoach* (1939). This was the film that would launch film legend, John Wayne, to stardom. Her portrayal of the dance hall girl, "Dallas," was electric and the on-screen chemistry between Wayne and Trevor was undeniable. The pair would go on to appear in three more films, *Allegheny Uprising* (1939), *Dark Command* (1940), and *The High and the Mighty* (1954) for which she would be nominated for another best supporting actress Oscar. Wayne and Trevor remained good friends the remainder of their lives, and lived for many years just steps away from one another in Newport Beach, California.

Did You Know?

Trevor appeared in numerous crime dramas in the 1940s and was dubbed the "Queen of Film Noir" for her on-screen bad girl image. Her best supporting actress Oscar is on display at the University of California, Irvine's Theater for the Performing Arts Center. Her stepson is billionaire developer Donald Bren who is chairman of the Irvine Company.

In 1948, she made her on-screen performance in *Key Largo;* in it she portrayed the boozy and heart wrenching pathetic night club owner Gaye Dawn. This performance won Trevor the 1949 best supporting actress Academy Award. Though her film career was a success, her private life was often in shambles. She was married three times. Her son Charles Bren was killed in a plane crash in 1978. Her third husband, noted film producer and land developer Milton Bren, died from a brain tumor the following year. Trevor never fully recovered from these traumas, and she herself suffered from debilitating arthritis. During the 1970s, she served as chairwoman of the Orange County Arthritis Foundation and also contributed to other charitable organizations. Additionally, she helped U. C. Irvine's performing arts department. In tribute to the actress, the School of Arts on campus is named in her honor. On April 8, 2000, at the age of ninety, screen legend Claire Trevor-Bren died from complications of an upper respiratory ailment at Hoag Hospital in Newport Beach.

Claire Trevor's cremated remains were scattered at sea off the Coast of Orange County.

John Huston

(August 5, 1906 – August 28, 1987)

"Tales of my toughness are exaggerated. I never killed an actor."

~John Huston

One of the most eccentric and multi-talented actor/director/writers of the Golden Age of Cinema, John Marcellus Huston was born on August 5, 1906 in Nevada, Missouri. He is the son of Oscar winning actor, Walter Huston. John's parents separated when he was three and the young Huston divided his time between his two parents. John had an adventuresome spirit, and at the age of nineteen enlisted in the Mexican army, where he spent two years in the cavalry. Returning to New York after his enlistment expired; Huston tried his hand at writing and then traveled to Hollywood with his father. His first film writing credit was *A House Divided* (1931), a film in which his father was starring.

Tragedy struck in the early evening of September 25, 1933, while driving his car, Huston struck and killed young actress Tosca Roulien (the wife of Brazilian actor Raoul Roulien) who was crossing Sunset Boulevard at Gardner Street in Hollywood. There was suspicion that Huston may have been driving under the influence of alcohol at the time of the accident but this was quickly ruled out with the help and influence of MGM studio head Louis B. Mayer. After a brief coroner's inquest held on September 27, 1933, Huston was quietly absolved of any blame for the accident. Following this incident, Huston left Hollywood for a brief period, returning in the late 1930s; when he helped write screen plays for numerous films such as *Jezebel* (1938), *Juarez* (1939), *Sergeant York* (1941), and *High Sierra* (1941).

Did You Know?

Huston's daughter is Oscar award-winning actress Anjelica Huston. He and his father, Walter, were the first father/son duo to win an Academy Award and in his youth, John was an amateur light weight boxing champion in California.

Huston made his motion picture directorial debut in 1941 with the classic film, *The Maltese Falcon*. It was this film that launched two careers, Huston's and

Humphrey Bogart's. Huston's acting/directing/ writing career spanned five decades (1929-1988); as an actor he appeared in over fifty films, primarily as an extra or as a narrator. Acting credits included:

- *Casino Royale* (1967)
- *Battle for the Planet of the Apes* (1973)
- *Chinatown* (1974)
- *The Wind and the Lion* (1975)

As a director, Huston made forty-seven films, some of which have become all-time classics; his directorial film credits include:

- *Key Largo* (1948)
- *The Misfits* (1961)
- *The Night of the Iguana* (1964)
- *Casino Royale* (1967)
- *The Life and Times of Judge Roy Bean* (1972)

Huston was nominated for an astounding fourteen Academy Awards during his film career; one for best actor in a supporting role for:

- *The Cardinal* (1963)

... eight for writing:

- *Dr. Ehrlich's Magic Bullet* (1940)
- *The Maltese Falcon* (1941)
- *Sergeant York* (1941)
- *The Asphalt Jungle* (1950)

- *The African Queen* (1951)
- *Heaven Knows, Mr. Allison* (1957)
- *The Man Who Would be King* (1975)
- *Prizzi's Honor* (1985)

... and five for best director:

- *The Asphalt Jungle* (1950)
- *The African Queen* (1951)
- *Moulin Rouge* (1952)

He won the 1949 Academy Award for best director and writing for his film, *The Treasure of the Sierra Madre* (1948), a movie in which his father, Walter Huston won for best supporting actor.

As a film director, John Huston was able to tell an effective story and he had a gift for capturing the raw emotion between people and his actors. Many of his films have become legendary classics. He died on August 28, 1987, at a rental home in Newport, Rhode Island from emphysema. He had been in ill health for almost a decade, first suffering a near fatal aortic aneurysm in 1977, and then developed respiratory problems, due to a lifelong smoking habit that left the rough and tumble director wheel chair bound. Even with these debilitating illnesses, Huston continued to work right up until his death.

John Huston's final resting place is at Hollywood Forever Cemetery, Los Angeles in the Garden of Legends section, lot 6 on the west side of the lake.

Director John Huston's grave at Hollywood Forever Cemetery.

The Twenty-Second
Academy Awards Ceremony
"Home, Sweet Home"

The Academy Award ceremony honoring the best films of 1949 was held on March 23, 1950, at the Pantages Theater, Hollywood, California, with actor Paul Douglas serving as the master of ceremonies. The Oscars would finally have a semi-permanent home at the ornate Pantages Theater. In the previous twenty years, the event had been held at eight different venues. The next ten years (1950-1960), the grand award spectacle would have a proper home.

This year's ceremony marked a return to Hollywood glamour of bygone years and almost all of the nominees chose to attend, even though the winners were very predictable. Though not a night of upsets, the award show was still deemed a great success. The best picture of the year went to the political melodrama, *All the Kings Men* (1949), based on the novel by Robert Penn Warren, which fictionalized the life and times of flamboyant Louisiana Governor Huey Long. This film would garner three of the top six Oscars, including best picture, actor and supporting actress.

Nominees and Winners

Best Actor
Kirk Douglas, **Broderick Crawford**, Gregory Peck, Richard Todd, and John Wayne

Best Actress
Jeanne Crain, Susan Hayward, **Olivia de Havilland**, Deborah Kerr, and Loretta Young

Best Supporting Actor
John Ireland, **Dean Jagger**, Arthur Kennedy, Ralph Richardson, and James Whitmore

Best Supporting Actress
Ethel Barrymore, Celeste Holm, Elsa Lanchester, and **Mercedes McCambridge**

Best Director
Joseph L. Mankiewicz, Carol Reed, Robert Rossen, William A. Wellman, and William Wyler

The Twenty-Second Academy Awards, March 23, 1950 at the Pantages Theater. *Courtesy of the Bruce Torrence Hollywood photograph Collection*

Broderick Crawford

(December 9, 1911 – April 26, 1986)

The husky, gravelly voiced actor of both film and television was born William Broderick Crawford on December 9, 1911, in Philadelphia, Pennsylvania. Born into a venerable acting family, his parents, Lester and Helen Crawford, were successful vaudevillian performers. His mother excelled in comedic roles on stage and film. Broderick's successful career in show business began on the Broadway stage in 1937's *Of Mice and Men*. In that same year, he ventured to Hollywood and appeared in his first motion picture, *Woman Chases Man* (1937). In a film and television career that spanned over four decades (1937-1982), Crawford appeared in over eighty feature films that included:

- *Ambush* (1939)
- *Beau Geste* (1939)
- *Slightly Honorable* (1940)
- *The Black Cat* (1941)
- *North to the Klondike* (1942)
- *Larceny, Inc.* (1942)
- *Black Angel* (1946)
- *A Kiss in the Dark* (1949)
- *Lone Star* (1952)
- *Born Yesterday* (1950)
- *The Last Posse* (1953)

Crawford was not the typical Hollywood leading-man type with a deep voice, large, and burly physique. He primarily played supporting roles as tough guys in "B" westerns.

In 1949, Crawford was not a big box office star. Director Robert Rosen was casting the lead role for the film, *All the Kings Men*, a film adaptation of Robert Penn Warren's fictionalized account of the life of flamboyant Louisiana politician, Huey Long. Rosen was not looking for a big star for his film. On the contrary, all he needed was an actor like Crawford, whose unknown stature, powerful build, and raspy voice, fit the persona of Willie Stark (AKA Huey Long). For this role, Crawford won the best lead actor Academy Award for 1949.

Crawford was unable to follow up the success of *All the Kings Men*, and his film career slowed. In 1955, he got another big break, this time on the small screen, playing one of the most memorable and legendary roles in television history that of Chief Dan Mathews in *Highway Patrol* (1955-1959). Crawford successful television career lasted for twenty-plus years. On April 26, 1986, Broderick Crawford died after suffering a massive stroke at the Eisenhower Medical Center in Palm Springs, California. The actor had been ill for several years prior to his death.

Broderick Crawford is buried at Ferndale Cemetery in Johnstown, New York.

Left to right: Jimmy Stewart, Olivia de Havilland, Broderick Crawford, and Jane Wyman, winners of Oscars on March 24, 1950. *Courtesy of the Herald Examiner Collection/ Los Angeles Public Library*

Olivia de Havilland

Best actress Oscar winner of 1949, Olivia de Havilland is still living and today resides in Paris, France having retired from Hollywood in the late 1980's after a long and illustrious film career.

Dean Jagger

(November 7, 1903 – February 5, 1991)

The award-winning character actor that was known for his firm but kindly demeanor was born Ira Dean Jagger on November 7, 1903, in Lima, Ohio. At the age of nineteen, after dropping out of Washburn College in Greencastle, Indiana, Jagger traveled to Chicago in pursuit of an acting career. After studying at the Chicago Conservatory of Drama, he began a successful run in the theater, appearing in numerous stage productions throughout the 1920s. Then in 1929, Jagger made his motion picture film debut in what would be one of Hollywood's last silent films, *The Woman from Hell*, starring Mary Astor. The tall and lanky actor was known as a consummate performer who rarely took the lead in any of his more than 130 film and television roles. In an award-winning show business career that spanned over five decades (1929-1987), Jagger's most memorable film credits include:

- *It's a Great Life* (1935)
- *Woman in Distress* (1937)
- *The North Star* (1943)
- *Alaska* (1944), *Rawhide* (1951)
- *The Robe* (1953)
- *White Christmas* (1954)
- *Bad Day at Black Rock* (1955)
- *King Creole* (1958)
- *The Nun's Story* (1959)
- *Elmer Gantry* (1960)

In 1949, Jagger won the Oscar for best supporting actor for his performance as the stoic Major Stovall in the World War II drama, *Twelve O'Clock High*.

Although most of career was spent on the large screen, Jagger did make numerous television show appearances, most notably *Mr. Novak* (1963-1965) for which he won an Emmy award (1965) for his portrayal of the affable High School principal, Albert Vane. Retiring from show business in 1987, Jagger spent the remaining years of his life in seclusion. He died in his sleep from a heart attack on February 5, 1991, at his home in Santa Monica, California. At the time of his death the actor had also been battling a severe case of the flu.

Dean Jagger is buried at the Lakewood Memorial Park in Hughson, California, in the North Hyland lawn section.

Mercedes McCambridge

(March 16, 1916 or 1918? – March 2, 2004)

The versatile and award-winning character actress of stage, screen, television, and radio was born Carlotta Mercedes Agnes McCambridge on March 16, 1916 in Joliet, Illinois. In 1936, while studying English and theater at Mundelein College in north suburban Chicago, Mercedes caught the eye of an NBC radio program director. During the late 1930s and early 1940s, McCambridge had roles in numerous popular radio programs such as *Dick Tracy*, *Inner Sanctum*, *The Thin Man*, and *Bulldog Drummond*. Throughout the middle 1940s, she appeared in numerous Broadway productions of varying success.

In 1949, she got her big break in motion pictures and in her debut performance won an Oscar for best supporting actress in the role of the hard-nosed and manipulative political aide, Sadie Burke in *All the Kings Men*. In a career that spanned nearly four decades from 1949 to 1988, she appeared in over twenty feature films and numerous television programs; her feature film credits include:

- *Johnny Guitar* (1954)
- *A Farewell to Arms* (1957)
- *Touch of Evil* (1958)
- *Suddenly, Last Summer* (1959)
- *Cimarron* (1960)
- *The Other Side of the Wind* (1972)
- *Airport 79'* (1979)

In 1956, she was nominated for a second best supporting actress Academy Award for her portrayal of Liz Benedict, the strong willed older sister of Rock Hudson's character in *Giant* (1956). She worked continuously in film, television, and Broadway her entire adult life and even earned a Tony Award nomination in 1972 for *The Love Suicide at Schofield Barracks*. While her film career did not live up to the high levels of expectations that were initially promised with her debut Oscar win, she remained quite satisfied with how her career evolved.

Did You Know?
McCambridge was the voice of the demon that possessed Linda Blair's character in *The Exorcist* (1973); she was reluctant to take the role, but was eventually persuaded by Orson Welles.

In 1987, tragedy struck, when her only son, John Lawrence Markle, killed his wife and two daughters in a murder suicide. She would battle alcoholism her entire adult life, and even testified before the U.S. Senate subcommittee on alcoholism and narcotics in 1969. She was married and divorced twice. In the mid-1980s, she retired from show business. McCambridge then moved to the seaside town of La Jolla, California. She died on March 2, 2004, of natural causes while living at a local assisted living facility. McCambridge had no known survivors.

Mercedes McCambride's remains were cremated and scattered at sea near San Diego.

Ray Milland and Mercedes McCambridge. *Courtesy of the Herald Examiner Collection/ Los Angeles Public Library*

Joseph Leo Mankiewicz

(February 11, 1909 – February 5, 1993)

The humorous writer turned director who won Oscars for both disciplines was born on February 11, 1909, in Wilkes-Barre, Pennsylvania. Initially, Mankiewicz wanted to be a psychiatrist but failed miserably in the course work at Columbia University. Eventually, he graduated from the university with a degree in liberal arts. After college he worked for a short period of time as a news correspondent in Berlin, Germany, for the *Chicago Tribune*. He relocated to Hollywood and began to write for films. In a show business career that spanned over forty years (1929-1972), Mankiewicz is credited with writing and/or directing over fifty films that include:

- *Alice in Wonderland* (1933, writing)
- *Manhattan Melodrama* (1934, writing)
- *The Ghost and Mrs. Muir* (1947, directing)
- *Guys and Dolls* (1951, writing and directing)
- *The Quiet American* (1958, writing and directing)
- *Cleopatra* (1963, writing and directing)
- *The Honey Pot* (1967, writing and directing)

His films were varied from classic adaptations to musicals to epics; he was a master in the use of flashbacks and clever dialogue.

He was nominated for ten Academy awards for writing, directing, and producing the films:

- *Skippy* (1931, nominated, writing)
- *The Philadelphia Story* (1940, nominated best picture, producer)
- *No Way Out* (1950, nominated, writing)
- *5 Fingers* (1952, nominated, director)
- *The Barefoot Contessa* (1954, nominated, writing)
- *Sleuth* (1972, nominated director)

In 1950, Mankiewicz won Oscars for directing and writing for the film, *A Letter to Three Wives* (1949) and he repeated this double triumph again in 1951 with the film, *All About Eve* (1950).

Disgruntled with the quality of films being produced in Hollywood, Mankiewicz retired from show business after directing the 1972 film, *Sleuth*. Settling into a home in Bedford, New York, he lived the last twenty years of his life in solitude. The acclaimed writer/director died on February 5, 1993 from a heart attack at his home.

Mankiewicz is buried at the Saint Mathews Episcopal Churchyard Cemetery in Bedford, New York.

Did You Know?

Mankiewicz is the only writer/director in the history of the Oscars to win for both disciplines in consecutive years (1950 and 1951). He is credited with writing the immortal lines, "Fasten your seat belts. It's going to be a bumpy night," which were spoken by actress Bette Davis in the film, *All About Eve* (1950). On why he started directing Mankiewicz said, "I felt the urge to direct, because I couldn't stomach what was being done with what I wrote." And he once called actress Katharine Hepburn, "the most experienced amateur actress in the world."

Epilogue
"New Hollywood" and the Decline of the Studio System

As the decade of the 1950s dawned, the heyday of the studio system began to rapidly decline. The studios began to lose their power over the stars and the films they created. The movie moguls who loomed large over the industry from 1927 to 1950 were either dead, dying, or were out of touch with the new emerging way of film making. The Golden Age of American Cinema was over and a transitional period developed during this decade that would eventually led to the "New Hollywood" era of film making (1960 to 1980).

What truly caused the demise of the studio system? Suddenly, and without warning, millions of people stopped going to the movies. Attendance sank from 80 million per week in 1946 to 60 million per week in 1948, and no studio fared worse than the grandest of the all, Metro-Goldwyn-Mayer. Long the biggest and richest studio in Hollywood, MGM suffered grievously from these financial blows. The studio had a gross income of $18 million the first twelve months after the war, but that declined to $4 million during the physical year of September 1947 to September 1948, and led to a net defect of some $6 million.

Four factors directly led to the decline of Hollywood's golden age: the introduction of television, which by the 1950s was beginning its own "golden age," the blacklisting of artists based on their alleged membership in or sympathy toward the American Communist party, the ability of actors to become "free agents," and a final blow came in 1948, when antitrust suits were filed against the major studios.

The most important event in Hollywood's golden age, attracted remarkably little attention at the time and didn't even take place in Hollywood. In 1948, the U.S. Justice Department persuaded the U.S. Supreme Court that the whole Hollywood system, all those rich and powerful studios and their highly paid executives were actually a criminal conspiracy.

The controversy dated back almost to the beginning of the movie business. As early as 1921, the Federal Trade Commission was investigating such Hollywood practices as block-booking and blind-selling. The producers, many of whom had started out as half-hearted opponents of the patent holders, now insisted on their own right to protect their interests.

February of 1948, Attorney General Thomas Clark appeared before the Supreme Court to argue once again that the studios must divest themselves of their theater chains. There was no other way, he claimed, "to effectively pry open to competition the channels of trade in the industry." The Justice Department had already submitted a petition to the Court arguing that its plea was not just a matter of free trade in the movie business but of free trade in ideas. "The content of films, regardless of who produces them or exhibits them, must necessarily be conditioned to some extent by the prejudices and moral attitudes of those who control the channels of distribution," the Justice Department brief said. "Only by assurance that the distribution field is open to all may the fullest diversity of film content be had."

"The major studios were not willing or not able to permit such diversity," the Justice Department said. "On the contrary, their past efforts had consisted of creating and maintaining a control of the film market expressly designed to prevent any views other than their own. Such a past, gives little hope that they will in the future encourage production of the wide verity of films needed to satisfy the wide variety of tastes possessed by the potential American film audiences, rather than a standardized mass product adapted to profitable exhibition in a controlled market."

In the midst of this rather confused situation, The Supreme Court spent three months reflecting on the Justice department's demand for "the fullest diversity of film content." Then it declared on May of 1948 that the Hollywood system was indeed a conspiracy, and that it would finally order the breakup that Thurma Arnold, chief of the FBI's anti-trust division, had requested before the war. "It is clear, so far as the five major studios are concerned, that the aim of the conspiracy was exclusionary, i.e., that it was designed to strengthen their hold on the exhibition field," said the seven to one opinion written by Justice William O. Douglas. In other words, the conspiracy had monopoly in exhibition as one of its goals.

In October, the Justice Department announced once again that it wanted the five major studios to give up their interests in some 1,400 movie theaters. It served notice on Paramount, Loew's, RKO, Warner's, and Fox that this would be its position when the New York District Court took up the case. Among the alleged conspirators, the one who cracked was, of all people, Howard Hughes. RKO told the federal authorities at the end of October that it would give up the battle and sell off its interest in 241 theaters within a year. Ten days later, Loew's also surrendered, and the others followed suit. A consent decree was approved by the Justice Department, the studios, and the court. Though it would take another year for the theaters to be sold, and still longer for the studios to realize the devastating implications of what had happened to them. The golden age that Hollywood had founded on a so-called "conspiracy" was coming to an end.

Many great films were made since the 1948 Supreme Court decision. But have motion pictures really gotten better? With the American Film Institute's recent announcement of their top 100 films, one needs only a passing glance to see that the bulk of them were produced by the major studios, during Hollywood's golden age. It is doubtful that the studios could have survived even had they been able to hold on to their theaters. As audiences dwindled, the studios had little choice but to liquidate their holdings. The dreaded seven-year contracts that the studios imposed on their actors and artistic people were being challenged. One by one the great movie studios began to fragment. MGM was bought by Kirk Kerkorian, a hotel magnate. Warner Brothers was eaten up my Seven Arts, and finally by the Kinney Corporation. Paramount was acquired by the Gulf & Western Company. MCA took over Universal. Harry Cohn's Columbia was acquired by Coca-Cola.

The great empires had crumbled. The pinnacles of power had diminished. What remained was an idea, a truth that in our minds, at least those of us who cherish the great classic period, will never vanish. And what we take away is a constellation of values, images, and attitudes, a history and a mythology that is part of our culture and consciousness.

Appendix A

Louis B. Mayer

Louis B. Mayer

(July 12, 1884 or

July 4, 1884? – October 29, 1957)

"I want to make beautiful pictures about beautiful people."

"What do we need another galoot for? We've already got Wallace Beery."
(Upon finding out that Irving Thalberg had hired
Spencer Tracy to join MGM)
Louis B. Mayer

If Clark Gable was the "King of Hollywood," then Louis B. Mayer was its "Emperor." Born Ezemiel Mayer on July 12, 1884, in Minsk, Belarus, Ukraine, his parents fled to Canada to avoid Jewish prosecution. Mayer grew up in great poverty and held very few found memories of his childhood. In his early adulthood, he had to scrap and claw to make even the most meager of living. In 1904, Mayer moved to Boston, where he got involved in burlesque theaters. He saved all his money and eventually bought a theater of his own. When motion pictures became all the rage, Mayer added it to his theater.

In 1915, Mayer hit the big time when he acquired the U.S. rights to D.W. Griffiths legendary film, *The Birth of a Nation* (1915). He saw that money could be made in film production and moved to Hollywood. He, along with good friend Irving Thalberg, set about to create a successful and profitable production company called Louis B. Mayer Productions, which specialized in low-budget melodramas.

In 1924, Marcus Loew, the owner of an up-and-coming theater empire, needed someone to head his newly created film production company, which had been merged from Metro Pictures and Samuel Goldwyn Pictures. The end result was Metro-Goldwyn-Mayer of which Louis B. Mayer was named vice-president of production. Mayer and Thalberg worked feverishly to

create a profitable and productive film studio. Films such as *Ben-Hur: Tale of the Christ* (1925) and *The Big Parade* (1925) were early successes.

Did You Know?
Mayer did not think highly of television and when told that it would be a serious competitor to motion pictures, he stated, "That's crap. Our position has never been more secure. Who in hell is going to look at those pigmy screens?"

Left to right: Harry Rapf, Louis B. Mayer, and Irving Thalberg. *Courtesy of the Herald Examiner Collection/ Los Angeles Public Library*

MGM was slow to adapt to talking pictures due to the monumental task of converting theaters to sound. But Thalberg and Mayer were able to create financially successful films with stars such as Jean Harlow, Joan Crawford, Norma Shearer, Myrna Loy, Clark Gable, William Powell, and Spencer Tracy. Throughout the decade of the 1930s, MGM studios continued to advance and by the end of the decade was the leading studio in Hollywood with everything culminating in 1939 with *Gone with the Wind* (1939). Mayer was known to be very manipulative and toyed with his actor's emotions. He was a master at reading peoples weaknesses and capitalized on them. While still maintaining a facade of paternalism and cunning, he saw MGM studios profitability rise year after year.

By 1948, due to the introduction of television and changing public tastes, MGM suffered a considerable drop-off in its success. The glory days of MGM as well as other studios were also over because of a Supreme Court decision that severed the connection between film studios and the movie theaters that showed their films. The MGM corporate office in New York decided that Dore Schary, a writer and producer recently hired from RKO Pictures, might be able to turn the tide. In 1951, MGM had gone three years without a major Academy Award, which provoked further conflict. Under orders to control costs and hire "a new Thalberg," Mayer hired writer and producer Schary as production chief. Schary, who was twenty years Mayer's junior, preferred message pictures in contrast with Mayer's taste for "wholesome" films. In 1951, Schenck fired Mayer from the post he'd held for twenty-seven years. The firing reportedly came after Mayer called New York and issued an ultimatum—"It's either me, or Schary." Mayer tried to stage a boardroom coup but failed and largely retired from public life.

Mayer was not ready for retirement, nor was he ready for "the New Hollywood" of the 1950s. For the next six years, he dabbled in real estate, and a few independent film productions, but basically he just sat back and watched as the mighty MGM studios fell into rapid decline. He always dreamed of a return to prominence, but on October 29, 1957, Mayer died at the UCLA Medical Center after a long battle with leukemia. His funeral service was held at the Wilshire Temple on October 31, 1957; in attendance were over 2,000 mourners that included film stars Fred Astaire, James Stewart, Norma Shearer, Jimmy Durante, and Jack Haley. Actress Jeanette MacDonald sang "Ah Sweet Mystery of Life," and actor Spencer Tracy read the eulogy. Tracy stated, "In Genesis we are told that there were giants in those days. We have giants in these days too but only rarely. Here was a giant indeed… Louis B. Mayer, a man of great stature. He stands head and shoulders rising above the mystic memory of Hollywood's past."

Mayer is interred at Home of Peace Cemetery, East Los Angeles in the mausoleum, Corridor of Immortality, crypt 405.

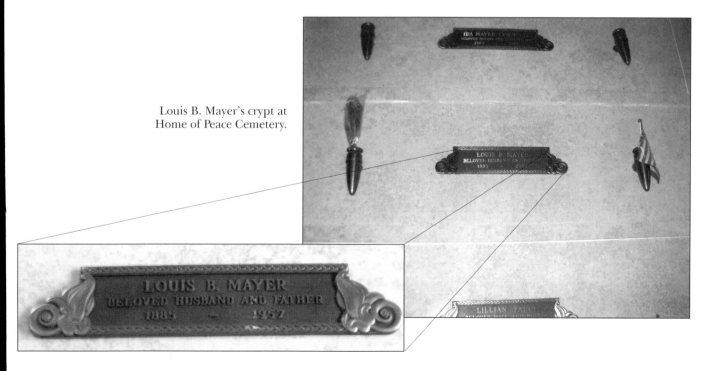

Louis B. Mayer's crypt at Home of Peace Cemetery.

Appendix B
The Original Thirty-Six Members of
the Academy of Motion Picture Arts and Sciences

Actors

Richard Barthelmess
(5/9/1895 – 8/17/1963)
Ferncliff Cemetery, Hartsdale, NY
Mausoleum, unit 8, alcove BB, column B, niche 1

Jack Holt
(5/31/1888 – 1/18/1951)
Los Angeles National Cemetery, Los Angeles, CA
Section 107, row A, grave 19

Conrad Nagel
(3/16/1897 – 2/24/1970)
Cremated, ashes given to family location unknown

Milton Sills
(1/12/1882 – 9/15/1930)
Rosehill Cemetery, Chicago, IL
Section 111, lot 38

Douglas Fairbanks, Sr.
(5/23/1883 – 12/12/1939)
Hollywood Forever Cemetery, Hollywood, CA
Reflecting pool adjacent to the cathedral mausoleum

Harold Lloyd
(4/20/1893 – 3/8/1971)
Forest Lawn, Glendale, CA
Great Mausoleum, Begonia Corridor

Mary Pickford
(4/9/1892 – 5/29/1979)
Forest Lawn, Glendale, CA
Garden of Memory

Directors

Cecil B. DeMille
(8/12/1881 – 1/21/1959)
Hollywood Forever Cemetery, Hollywood, CA
Garden of Legends, section 8, lot 50, north side of the lake

Frank Lloyd
(2/2/1888 – 8/10/1960)
Forest Lawn, Glendale, CA
Ascension lawn, lot 8438

Henry King
(1/24/1886 – 6/29/1982)
Holy Cross Cemetery, Culver City, CA

Fred Niblo, Sr.
(1/6/1874 – 11/11/1948)
Forest Lawn, Glendale, CA
Great Mausoleum, Columbarium of the Dawn, niche 30247

John M. Stahl
(1/21/1886 – 1/12/1950)
Forest Lawn, Glendale, CA

Raoul A. Walsh
(3/11/1887 – 12/31/1980)
Assumption Catholic Cemetery, Simi Valley, CA

Lawyers

Edwin Loeb
Unknown

George W. Cohen
Unknown

Producers

Fred Beetson
Unknown

Charles H. Christie
(4/13/1880 – 10/1/1955)
Hollywood Forever Cemetery, Hollywood, CA
Garden of Legends, #178

Sid Grauman
(3/17/1879 – 3/5/1950)
Forest Lawn, Glendale, CA
Great Mausoleum, Memorial Terrace, Sanctuary of
Benediction

Milton E. Hoffman
Unknown

Jesse L. Lasky
(9/13/1880 – 1/13/1958)
Hollywood Forever Cemetery, Hollywood, CA
Abby of the Palms, Sanctuary of Light, Corridor G-3,
Crypt 2196

M. C. Levee
Unknown

Louis B. Mayer
(7/4/1885 – 10/29/1957)
Home of Peace Memorial Park, East Los Angeles,
CA
Mausoleum, Corridor of Immortality, #405

Joseph M. Schenck
(12/25/1878 – 10/25/1961)
Maimonides Cemetery, Brooklyn, NY

Irving Thalberg
(3/30/1899 – 9/14/1936)
Forest Lawn, Glendale, CA
Great Mausoleum, Sanctuary of Benediction

Harry Warner
(12/12/1881 – 7/25/1958)
Home of Peace Memorial Park, East Los Angeles,
CA
Family Mausoleum

Jack Warner
(8/2/1892 – 9/9/1978)
Home of Peace Memorial Park, East Los Angeles,
CA
Jack Warner Garden plot

Harry Rapf
(10/16/1880 – 2/6/1949)
Home of Peace Memorial Park, East Los Angeles,
CA
Chapel Mausoleum, Corridor of Immortality, C-104
SW

Technical

Arthur Ball
(8/16/1894 – 8/27/1951)
Westwood Memorial Park, Los Angeles, CA

Cedric Gibbons
(3/23/1893 – 7/26/1960)
Calvary Cemetery, Los Angeles, CA
Lawn H, lot 117

Roy J. Pomeroy
Unknown

Writers

Joseph Farnham
(12/1/1884 – 6/2/1931)
Forest Lawn, Glendale, CA
Whispering Pines lawn, lot 1039, space 7

Benjamin Glazer
(5/7/1887 – 3/18/1956
Unknown

Jeanie MacPherson
(5/18/1887 – 8/26/1946)
Hollywood Forever Cemetery, Hollywood, CA
Chapel Colonnade, west corridor, south wall, niche
T-2

Bess Meredyth
(2/12/1890 – 7/13/1969)
Unknown

Carey Wilson
(5/19/1889 – 2/1/1962)
Hollywood Forever Cemetery, Hollywood, CA
Garden of Legends, lot 66

Frank E. Woods
(1860 – 5/1/1939)
Hollywood Forever Cemetery, Hollywood, CA
Chapel of the Psalms, north wall

Appendix C
Cemetery Addresses

1ˢᵗ Cemetery of Athens
Anapafseos and Iioupoleos Streets, Athens, Greece

All Saints Churchyard Cemetery
Uxbridge Road, Harrow Weald, England

Angelus Rosedale Cemetery
1831 W. Washington Boulevard, Los Angeles, CA 90007

Arlington National Cemetery
Arlington, VA 22211

Belmont Memorial Park
201 Teilman Avenue, Fresno, CA 93706

Calvary Cemetery
4201 Whittier Boulevard Los Angeles, CA 90023

Cedar Hill Cemetery
453 Fairfield Avenue, Harford, CT 06114

Chapel of the Pines
1605 S. Catalina Street, Los Angeles, CA

Cochella Valley Public Cemetery
82925 52ⁿᵈ Avenue, Thermal, CA 92274

Deansgrange Cemetery
Grange Rd., Blackrock, County Dublin, Ireland

East Fincheley Cemetery (formerly Saint Marylebonne)
East End Road, East Fincheley, England

Ferncliff Cemetery
280 Secor Road, Hartsdale, NY 10530

Ferndale Cemetery
545 N. Perry Street, Johnstown, NY 12095

Forest Lawn (Cathedral City)
69855 E. Ramon Road, Cathedral City, CA 92234

Forest Lawn (Glendale)
1712 S. Glendale Avenue, Glendale, CA 91205

Forest Lawn (Hollywood Hills)
6300 Forest Lawn Drive, Los Angeles, CA 90068

Gate of Heaven Cemetery
10 W. Stevens Avenue, Hawthorne, NY 10532

Mount Vernon Cemetery
3499 W. Lehigh Avenue, Philadelphia, PA 19132

Hollywood Forever Cemetery
6000 Santa Monica Boulevard, Los Angeles, CA 90038

Holy Cross Cemetery
5835 W. Slausen Avenue, Culver City, CA 90230

Lake View Cemetery
Commonwealth Road, Cochituate, MA

Lakewood Memorial Park
900 Santa Fe Avenue, Hughson, CA 95326

Lloyd-Jones Cemetery at Unity Chapel
6514 Hillside School Road, Spring Grove, WI 53588

Mount Auburn Cemetery
580 Mount Auburn St., Cambridge, MA 02138

Northern Cemetery (Norra Begravingsplaten)
Solna, Sweden

Oak Hill Cemetery
140 N. Highland Avenue, Nyack, NY 10960

Oakwood Memorial Park
22600 Lassen Street, Chatsworth, CA 91311

Parish of Saint Peter's Cemetery
Barbados

Sacred Heart Cemetery
168 Hill Street, Southampton, NY 11968

Saint Wolfgang Friedhof Cemetery
Salzburg, Austria

San Fernando Mission Cemetery
11150 Sepulveda Boulevard, Mission Hills, CA 91345

Santa Barbara Cemetery
901 Channel Drive, Santa Barbera, CA 93108

Sleepy Hollow Cemetery
540 N. Broadway, Sleepy Hollow, NY 10591

Sparkman-Hillcrest Memorial Park
7405 W. Northwest Highway, Dallas TX

Westwood Memorial Park
1218 Glendon Avenue, Los Angeles, CA 90024

Bibliography

Altman, Richard. *And the Envelope Please, A Quiz Book About the Academy Awards*. Philadelphia, Pennsylvania: J.B. Lippincott Company, 1978.

Barrow, Kenneth. *Mr. Chips: The Life of Robert Donat*. London: Mithuen Publishing, 1985.

Chandler, Charlotte. *Not the Girl Next Door: Joan Crawford a Personal Biography*. New York: Apple Theatre and Cinema Books, 2008.

Coleman, Terry. *Olivier: The Authorized Biography*. London: Bloomsbury Publishing, 2005.

Corey, Melinda & George Ochoa, eds. *The American Film Institute Desk Reference*. New York: Stonesong Press, 2002.

Edmonds, I.G. and Reiko Mimura. *The Oscar Directors*. San Diego, California: A.S. Barnes and Company, 1980.

Edwards, Anne. *Vivien Leigh, A Biography*. Philadelphia: Coronet Books, 1978.

Eliot, Mark. *Jimmy Stewart: A Biography*. New York: Random House, 2006.

Eyman, Scott. *Mary Pickford: America's Sweetheart*. New York: Donald Fine, Inc., 1990.

Goldstein, Steve. *LA's Graveside Companion, Where the VIP's RIP*. Atglen, Pennsylvania: Schiffer Publishing, 2009.

Hark, Ina Rae, ed. *American Cinema of the 1930's: Themes and Variations*. New Brunswick, New Jersey: Rutgers University Press, 2007.

Holden, Anthony. *Behind the Oscars: The Secret History of the Academy Awards*. New York: Simon & Schuster, 1993.

Jewell, Richard B. *The Golden Age of Cinema, Hollywood 1929-1945*. Malden, Maine: Blackwell Publishing, 2007.

Kaplan, Mike. Variety: *Who's Who in Show Business*. New York: Garland Publishing, Inc., 1983.

Katz, Ephrain. *The Film Encyclopedia*. 2nd ed. New York: Harper Collins, Inc., 1994.

Kinn, Gail and Jim Piazza. *The Academy Awards: The Complete Unofficial History*. New York: Black Dog and Leventhal Publishers, 2008.

Klien, Shelley. *Frankly, My Dear: Quips and Quotes from Hollywood*. New York: Barron's, 2006.

Lackmann, Ronald W. *Mercedes McCambridge: A Biography and Career Record*. North Carolina: McFarland & Company, 2005.

Leaming, Barbara. *Katharine Hepburn*. New York: Limelight, 2000.

McCambridge, Mercedes. *The Quality of Mercy: An Autobiography*. New York: The Berkley Publishing Group, 1982.

Milland, Ray. *Wide-Eyed in Babylon: An Autobiography*. New York: Morrow, Inc., 1974.

Monush, Barry. *The Encyclopedia of Hollywood Film Actors: From the Silent Era to 1965*. Milwaukee, WI: Hal Leonard Corporation, 2003.

O'Neil, Tom. *Movie Awards: The Ultimate, Unofficial Guide to the Oscars, Golden Globes, Critics, Guild and Indie Honors*. New York: The Berkley Publishing Group, 2003.

Parish, James Robert. *The Hollywood Book of Death*. New York: McGraw-Hill, 2002.

Peters, James Edward. *Arlington National Cemetery: Shrine to America's Heroes*. Bethesda, Maryland: Woodbine House, 2008.

Quirk, Lawrence J. *Fasten Your Seat Belts: The Passionate Life of Bette Davis*. New York: William Morrow, Inc, 1990.

Rogers, Ginger. *Ginger: My Story*. New York: Harper Collins, 1991.

Shipman, Robert. *The Great Movie Stars: The Golden Years*. London: MacDonald Press, 1989.

Simonet, Thomas. *Oscar: A Pictorial History of the Academy Awards*. Chicago: Contemporary Books, Inc., 1983.

Truitt, Evelyn Mack. *Who was Who on Screen*. 2nd ed. New York: R.R. Bowker Company, 1977.

Walker, Alexander. *Vivien: The Life of Viivien Leigh*. New York: Weiden & Nicholson, 1987.

Warren, Doug. *James Cagney: The Auhtorized Biography*. New York: St. Martin Press, 1983.

Wayne, Pilar, with Alex Thorleifson. *John Wayne: My Life with the Duke*. New York: McGraw Hill, 1987.

Wiley, Mason & Damien Bona. *Inside Oscar: The Unofficial History of the Academy Awards*. New York: Ballantine Books, 1988.

On the Web:

American Film Institute, www.afi.com
Find a Grave, www.findagrave.com by various contributors.
Internet Movie Database, www.imdb.com by various contributors.
Wikipedia, www.wikipedia.org by various contributors.

Newpapers:

The New York Times, various years and contributors
The Los Angeles Times, various years and contributors
The Orange County Register, various years and contributors

Photography Credits:

Index